The
RICE
SEEDLING
SUTRA

T0346733

Geshe Yeshe Thabkhe
Photo by Armen Elliott

The
RICE
SEEDLING
SUTRA

*Buddha's Teachings on
Dependent Arising*

Geshe Yeshe Thabkhe

TRANSLATED BY

Joshua and Diana Cutler

Wisdom

Wisdom Publications, Inc.
199 Elm Street
Somerville MA 02144 USA
wisdomexperience.org

Library of Congress Cataloging-in-Publication Data

Names: Thabkhe, Yeshe, 1930– author. | Cutler, Joshua W. C., translator. | Cutler, Diana, translator.
Title: The rice seedling sutra: an introduction to dependent arising / Geshe Yeshe Thabkhe; translated by Joshua Cutler and Diana Cutler.
Other titles: Tripiṭaka. Sūtrapiṭaka. Śālistambasūtra. English.
Description: Somerville, MA: Wisdom Publications, [2020] | Includes English translation of Śālistambasūtra. | Includes bibliographical references and index. |
Identifiers: LCCN 2019031235 (print) | LCCN 2019031236 (ebook) |
    ISBN 9781614296430 (paperback) | ISBN 9781614296447 (ebook)
Subjects: LCSH: Tripiṭaka. Sūtrapiṭaka. Śālistambasūtra—Criticism, interpretation, etc. |
    Pratītyasamutpāda. | Causation (Buddhism)
Classification: LCC BQ4240 .T49 2020 (print) | LCC BQ4240 (ebook) | DDC 294.3/85—dc23
LC record available at https://lccn.loc.gov/2019031235
LC ebook record available at https://lccn.loc.gov/2019031236

ISBN 978-1-61429-643-0   ebook ISBN 978-1-61429-644-7

24 23 22 21
5 4 3 2

Cover design by Phil Pascuzzo. Interior design by James D. Skatges.

"The Rice Seedling" translation is excerpted and adapted from *The Śālistamba Sūtra and Its Indian Commentaries*, translated by Jeffrey D. Schoening and published by Arbeitskreis für Tibetische und Buddhistische Studien Universität Wien in 1995. Revised translation © 2016 Jeffrey D. Schoening. Used by permission of Jeffrey D. Schoening.

Printed on acid-free paper that meets the guidelines for permanence and durability of the Production Guidelines for Book Longevity of the Council on Library Resources.

Printed in the United States of America.

Contents

Preface   vii

The Rice Seedling: A Mahayana Sutra   1
Translated by Jeffrey D. Schoening

1. How to Seek Reality by Means of Buddha's Teaching
   on Dependent Arising   13
2. Analysis of the Divine Creator   33
3. Is Dependently Arisen Production Actual Production?   55
4. How Phenomena Exist   73
5. The Trainings of the Three Types of Persons   87
6. Escaping the Wheel of Life   91
7. The Factors of Dependent Arising   113
8. How the Self Exists   127

Notes   145
Bibliography   153
Index   157
About the Author   161

Preface

The seed of the present book was planted when I started a Hindi translation of the great Indian scholar Kamalaśila's commentary on the *Rice Seedling Sutra* (*Śālistamba Sūtra*), which was published in 2010. For this publication I also wrote an introduction in Tibetan. The title I gave my introduction was "Dependent Arising, the King of Reasons Used to Distinguish the Ontological Status of All Things" (*Gnas lugs 'byed pa'i rigs pa'i rgyal po*). Usually an introduction would not require a title, but I wanted to emphasize the importance of the subject matter, dependent arising. I composed it as a commentary on the meaning of the sutra, not as a commentary on its words.

In the *Rice Seedling Sutra*, the Buddha explains to Śāriputra how things arise based on multiple causes and conditions. Likewise, the present work could not have come about without the contributions of many individuals. When I was working on the Hindi publication, I gave an explanatory reading of the Tibetan introduction to Joshua and Diana Cutler while residing at their Dharma center, the Tibetan Buddhist Learning Center in Washington, New Jersey. They in turn drafted an English translation based on my explanation, and Dr. Amy Miller edited their work. Loseling Geshe Dadul Namgyal contributed his English translation of two parts of the introduction and later offered his editing suggestions for the entire translation. Venerable Thubten Chodron, abbess of Sravasti Abbey in Newport, Washington, also edited the entire text, and she encouraged me to publish the translation because she noted that there is no such explanation in English of the Buddha's core teaching of dependent arising accompanied by many citations of original sources. I wish to thank them all for their help and encouragement.

When the manuscript of this English translation was almost ready to show a publisher, I thought that it needed a translation of the *Rice Seedling Sutra* to make it complete. As I was told that Jeffrey Schoening had already done an authoritative translation, I asked him if he would be willing to publish his translation along with my introduction. He agreed after determining that he would retranslate the sutra so that it was more appropriate for a general audience, taking my introduction's English translation into consideration. His revised translation begins this book.

A discourse on the Buddha's teachings traditionally begins by praising the source of the teachings, promising to compose the text, and stating the purpose of composing the text. Thus I began my introduction with the following verses of homage and intention:

You who taught dependent arising through your own understanding,
refuting the view of a divine creator of the world
and clarifying the correct mundane view and four seals,
O Supreme Master, please look after me always.

Though I have weak mental fortitude to analyze precisely
the meaning of the *Rice Seedling Sutra* spoken by that Master,
as I wish to be a fortunate person,
I will enthusiastically endeavor to offer this short introduction.

I did not compose this to show to scholars
nor to expand on the study of logic in the monasteries.
In hopes of assisting a few beginners,
I earnestly set forth this simply worded introduction to the best of my
    ability.

The Rice Seedling: A Mahayana Sutra

Translated by Jeffrey D. Schoening

The title in Sanskrit: *Ārya-śālistamba-nāma-mahāyāna-sūtra*
The title in Tibetan: *'Phags pa sā lu ljang pa zhes bya ba theg pa chen po'i mdo*

Homage to all the buddhas and bodhisattvas!

Thus I heard on one occasion when the Blessed One was staying at Rājagṛha on Vulture Peak Mountain together with a great assembly of monks, 1,250 monks, and very many bodhisattva great beings.

At that time the Venerable Śāriputra went to the promenade of Maitreya, the bodhisattva great being. On his arriving they exchanged many pleasantries, and having met, they sat together on a stone slab. Then the Venerable Śāriputra said this to the bodhisattva great being Maitreya, "Maitreya, here today the Blessed One, after looking at a rice seedling, spoke this sutra to the monks, 'Monks, he who sees dependent arising sees the Dharma; he who sees the Dharma sees the Buddha.' After saying that, the Blessed One said nothing more. Maitreya, what is the meaning of that sutra spoken by the Sugata? What is dependent arising? What is the Dharma? What is the Buddha? How does one see the Dharma if one sees dependent arising? How does one see the Buddha if one sees the Dharma?"

Once this was said, the bodhisattva great being Maitreya said this to the Venerable Śāradvatiputra: "Reverend Śāriputra, the Blessed One, the Lord of Dharma, the Omniscient One, said, 'Monks, he who sees dependent arising sees the Dharma; he who sees the Dharma sees the Buddha.' If, regarding that, you ask what dependent arising is, it is as follows. Because this exists, this occurs; because this arose, this arises; this is called *dependent arising*. That is, dependent on ignorance, conditioning factors occur; dependent on conditioning factors, consciousness; dependent on consciousness, name-and-form; dependent on name-and-form, the six sense-bases; dependent on the six sense-bases, contact; dependent on contact, feeling; dependent on feeling, craving; dependent on craving, grasping; dependent on grasping, becoming; dependent on becoming, birth; dependent on birth occur aging and death, sorrow, lamentation, misery, unhappiness, and conflict. This entire great heap of suffering occurs in that way. Likewise, with the cessation of ignorance, conditioning factors cease; with the cessation of conditioning factors, consciousness ceases; with the cessation of consciousness, name-and-form cease; with the cessation of name-and-form, the six sense-bases cease; with the cessation of the six sense-bases, contact ceases; with the cessation of contact, feeling ceases; with the cessation of feeling, craving ceases; with the cessation of craving, grasping ceases; with the cessation of grasping, becoming ceases; with the cessation of becoming, birth ceases; and the cessation of birth brings the cessation of aging and death, sorrow, lamentation, misery, unhappiness, and conflict. This entire great heap of suffering will cease in that way. This the Blessed One calls *dependent arising*.

"What is the Dharma? It is the noble eightfold path, namely: right view, right thought, right speech, right action, right livelihood, right effort, right mindfulness, and right concentration. This is called the noble eightfold path; and combining it with the attainment of the result and nirvāṇa, the Blessed One calls these the Dharma.

"Regarding that, what is the Buddha, the Blessed One? He is called Buddha because he comprehends all the dharmas; by means of the noble's eye of discriminating insight and the body of enlightened qualities, he is enlightened and sees the dharmas of the learner and the learned.[1]

"Regarding that, how is dependent arising seen? About this the Blessed One said, 'He who sees dependent arising as permanent, without life, free of life, just as it is, unerring, unborn, unarisen, not made, unconditioned, unobstructed, baseless, peaceful, fearless, not to be taken away, as an essential nature that is not pacified [sees the Dharma]; he who sees the Dharma also in a similar way as permanent, without life, free of life, just as it is, unerring, unborn, unarisen, not made, unconditioned, unobstructed, baseless, peaceful, fearless, not to be taken away, as an essential nature that is not pacified, realizes the noble Dharma; due to possessing perfect wisdom, [he] sees the Buddha as the unsurpassable body of enlightened qualities.'

"Objection: Why is it called *dependent arising*?

"Answer: It possesses causes and conditions and is not causeless [nor] conditionless. Therefore it is called *dependent arising*.

"Regarding that, the Blessed One briefly stated the defining characteristic of dependent arising:

[This] is the result of conditionedness: "Whether tathāgatas arise or not, this nature of dharmas remains."

up to:

This which is the nature, the stability of dharmas, the invariable principle of dharmas, the conformity to dependent arising, thusness, unerring thusness, unique thusness, verity, truth, unerringness, and the right.

"Furthermore, this dependent arising arises on the basis of two. What are the two? From dependence on causes and dependence on conditions. That also is to be seen as twofold: external and internal.

"Regarding that, what is the dependence on causes of external dependent arising? That is: from the seed a sprout, from the sprout a leaf, from the leaf a stalk, from the stalk a hollow stalk, from the hollow stalk a bud, from the bud a flower, from the flower a fruit. When there is no seed, the sprout will not arise; up to when there is no flower, the fruit will not arise. When there is a seed, the sprout will be produced; similarly, up to when there is a flower, the fruit will be produced.

"Regarding that, it does not occur to the seed, 'I produce the sprout.' It does not occur to the sprout, 'I was produced by the seed.' Similarly, up to it does not occur to the flower, 'I produce the fruit,' and it does not occur to the fruit, 'I was produced by the flower.' However, when there is a seed, the sprout is produced and appears; similarly, up to when there is a flower, the fruit will be produced and appear: thus is to be seen the dependence on causes of external dependent arising.

"How is dependence on conditions of external dependent arising to be seen? Because of the assemblage of the six elements. Because of the assemblage of what six elements? That is: from the assemblage of the earth, water, fire, air, space, and season elements is to be seen the dependence on conditions of external dependent arising.

"Regarding that, the earth element performs the function of supporting the seed. The water element moistens the seed. The fire element matures the seed. The air element opens the seed. The space element performs the function of not obstructing the seed. The season element performs the function of transforming the seed. Without these conditions, the sprout will not be produced from the seed. However, when the external earth element is not deficient—and likewise water, fire, air, space, and season are not deficient—all are assembled, should the seed cease, from that the sprout would be produced.

"Regarding that, it does not occur to the earth element, 'I perform the function of supporting the seed.' Similarly, it does not occur to the water element, 'I moisten the seed.' It does not occur to the fire element, 'I mature the seed.' It does not occur to the air element, 'I open the seed.' It does not occur to the space element, 'I perform the function of not obstructing the seed.' It does not occur to the season, 'I perform the function of transforming the seed.' It does not occur to the seed, 'I produce the sprout.' It does not occur to the sprout, 'I was produced by these conditions.' However, when these conditions exist and the seed ceases, a sprout will be produced. Similarly, up to: When the flower exists, a fruit also will be produced.

"And the sprout is not made by itself, not made by another, not made by both, not made by Īśvara, not transformed by time, not arisen from essential nature, nor born without a cause. However, the elements of earth, water, fire, air, space, and season having assembled, when the seed ceases, the sprout will be produced. Like that, dependence on conditions of external dependent arising is to be seen.

"Regarding that, external dependent arising is to be seen as fivefold. What five? Not eternalism, not annihilation, not transmigration, a great result arises from a small cause, and the continuity of what is similar to that.

"How is [external dependent arising] not eternalism? Because the sprout is one thing and the seed is another, precisely that which is the sprout is not the seed. After the seed has ceased, the sprout does not arise, and when the seed has not ceased, the sprout does not arise. Only at the moment the seed ceases does the sprout arise. Thus [external dependent arising] is not eternalism.

"How is it not annihilation? The sprout is not born from a seed that has already ceased, nor is it born from a seed that has not ceased. However, at the moment the seed ceases, the sprout arises in the same manner as the high and low ends of a balance beam. Therefore, [external dependent arising] is not annihilation.

"How is it not transmigration? Because the sprout is one thing and the seed another; precisely that which is the sprout is not the seed. Therefore [external dependent arising] is not transmigration.

"How does a great result arise from a small cause? From planting a small seed, a large fruit arises. Therefore, a great result arises from a small cause.

"[How is external dependent arising the continuity of what is similar to that?] Since the planted seed produces a similar fruit, there is continuity of what is similar to that. In that way, external dependent arising is to be seen as fivefold.

"In a similar way, internal dependent arising also arises on the basis of two. What are the two? Dependence on causes and dependence on conditions.

"Regarding that, what is the dependence on causes of internal dependent arising? It is as follows: 'Dependent on ignorance, conditioning factors' up to 'dependent on birth, aging and death.' If ignorance did not arise, the conditioning factors also will not become manifest. In this way up to, 'If birth did not arise, aging and death also will not become manifest.' Likewise, from 'Out of ignorance existing, conditioning factors will be produced' up to 'From birth existing, aging and death will be produced.'

"Regarding that, it does not occur to ignorance, 'I produce conditioning factors.' It does not occur to the conditioning factors, 'We were produced by ignorance.' Similarly up to it does not occur to birth, 'I produce aging and death,' and it does not occur to aging and death, 'We were produced by birth.' However, from 'Out of ignorance existing, conditioning factors are produced and become manifest,' similarly up to 'From birth existing, aging and death are produced and become manifest.' In that way, dependence on causes of internal dependent arising is to be seen.

"How is dependence on conditions of internal dependent arising to be seen? From the six elements assembling. From what six elements assembling? That is, from earth, water, fire, air, space, and consciousness elements assembling, dependence on conditions of internal dependent arising is to be seen.

"Regarding that, what is the earth element of internal dependent arising? That which, from bonding the body[2] together, produces the state of firmness is called the earth element. That which causes the body to hold together is called the water element. That which causes what is eaten, drunk, bitten, and tasted by the body to be digested is the fire element. That which causes the inhalation and exhalation of the body is called the air element. That which causes there to be an inner cavity of the body is the space element. That which produces the sprout of name-and-form of the body, assembles the group of five consciousnesses, and is the contaminated mental consciousness, in the manner of a reed bundle, is the consciousness element. Without these conditions, the body will not be born, but when the internal earth element is complete, and similarly the water, fire, air, space, and consciousness elements also are complete, from all those assembling, the body will be produced.

"Regarding that, it does not occur to the earth element, 'I, from bonding the body[3] together, produce the state of firmness.' It does not occur to the water element, 'I give the body cohesion.' It does not occur to the fire element, 'I digest what is eaten, drunk, bitten, and tasted by the body.' It does not occur to the air element, 'I perform the body's inhalations and exhalations.' It does not occur to the space element, 'I cause there to be the inner cavity of the body.' It does not occur to the consciousness element, 'I produce the name-and-form of the body.' It does not occur to the body, 'I was produced by these conditions.' Nevertheless, when these conditions exist, the body will be born.

"Regarding that, the earth element is not the self, not a being, not a life force, not a creature, not Manu's progeny, not Manu's descendant, not a woman, not a man, not a neuter, not I, not mine, and not of any other. Similarly, the water element, fire element, air element, space element, and consciousness element are not the self, not a being, not a life-force, not a creature, not Manu's progeny, not Manu's descendant, not a woman, not a man, not a neuter, not I, not mine, and not of any other.

"Regarding that, what is ignorance? The beliefs that these same six elements are a unit, a uniform mass, permanent, enduring, unchanging, pleasurable, a self, a being, a life-force, a creature, thriving, a human, an individual, Manu's progeny, Manu's descendant, 'I,' 'mine,' and various types of nescience such as that are called *ignorance*. Thus, because ignorance is present, desire, anger, and bewilderment proceed in relation to objects. Regarding that, desire, anger, and bewilderment with regard to objects are called the conditioning factors dependent on ignorance. Knowing entities individually is consciousness. The four appropriating aggregates arising together with consciousness are name-and-form. The sense organs that depend on name-and-form are the six sense-bases. The three factors assembling is contact. The contact experience is feeling. The attraction to feeling is craving. Increased craving is grasping. Karma, arising from grasping and producing rebirth, is becoming. The aggregation arising from that cause is birth. Following birth, the aggregation maturing is aging. Following aging, the aggregation perishing is death. The internal anguish of one dying, bewildered, and with strong grasping is sorrow. The lament that arises from sorrow is lamentation. The unpleasant experience associated with the group of five consciousnesses is misery. Mental suffering associated with mentation is unhappiness. And whatever other ancillary defilements such as that are called 'conflict.'

"Regarding that, because of great darkness, there is ignorance. Because of accomplishment, there are conditioning factors. Because it informs, consciousness. Because they support, name-and-form. Because they are a medium for arising, the six sense-bases. Because of contact, contact. Because of thirst, craving. Because of attachment, grasping. Because it produces rebirth, becoming. Because of the arising of the aggregation, birth. Because of the maturation of the aggregation, aging. Because of its disintegration, death. Because it causes sorrow, sorrow. Because of laments with words, lamentation. Because of harm to the body, misery. Because of harm to the mind, unhappiness. Because of defilement, conflict.

"Furthermore, not understanding and incorrectly knowing reality is nescience, which is ignorance.

"In that way, when ignorance exists, the threefold conditioning factors are produced: those leading to the wholesome, those leading to the unwholesome, and those leading to the immovable. Regarding that, from the conditioning factors leading to the wholesome arises just the consciousness leading to the wholesome; from the conditioning factors leading to the unwholesome arises just the consciousness leading to the unwholesome; from the conditioning factors leading to the immovable arises just the consciousness leading to the immovable. This is called 'dependent on conditioning factors, consciousness.'

"Consciousness arising together with the four formless aggregates and the form [aggregate] are called 'dependent on consciousness, name-and-form.' Because name-and-form develop, by means of the six sense-bases the performances of the functions occur; that is called 'dependent on name-and-form, the six sense-bases.' From the six sense-bases arise the six groups of contact; that is called 'dependent on the six sense-bases, contact.' Whatever type of contact arises, that type of feeling arises; that is called 'dependent on contact, feeling.' That which enjoys those types of feelings, that wishes, clings, and remains having clung, is called 'dependent on feeling, craving.' From enjoying, wishing, and remaining after having clung, and because of not abandoning the thought, 'May I not be separated from the beautiful nature and the pleasing nature,' this wish is called 'dependent on craving, grasping.' Thus wishing, the karma that produces rebirth arises by body, speech, and mind; that is called 'dependent on grasping, becoming.' The obtainment, the five aggregates born from that karma, is called 'dependent on becoming, birth.' The growth of aggregates produced from birth, the maturation, and the destruction is called 'dependent on birth, aging and death.'

"Thus this twelve-factor dependent arising, which arises from reciprocal causes and from reciprocal conditions, is not permanent, not impermanent, not conditioned, not unconditioned, not without causes, not without conditions, not an experiencer, not a waning dharma, not a perishing dharma, not a ceasing dharma, and in procession from beginningless time proceeds uninterruptedly like the flow of a river.

"While indeed this twelve-factor dependent arising, which arises from reciprocal causes and from reciprocal conditions, is not permanent, not impermanent, not conditioned, not unconditioned, not without causes, not without conditions, not an experiencer, not a waning dharma, not a perishing dharma, not a ceasing dharma, and in procession from beginningless time, uninterruptedly proceeds like the flow of a river; still, these four factors proceed by being the cause for the function that assembles those twelve factors of dependent arising. What are the four? They are ignorance, craving, karma, and consciousness.

"Thus consciousness is the cause with the essential nature of a seed. Karma is the cause with the essential nature of a field. Ignorance and craving are causes with the essential nature of defilement. Regarding that, karma and defilement produce the consciousness that is a seed. Regarding that, karma performs the function of a field for the consciousness that is a seed. Craving moistens the consciousness that is a seed. Ignorance sows the consciousness that is a seed. If these conditions do not exist, the consciousness that is a seed will not be produced.

"Regarding that, it does not occur to karma, 'I perform the function of the field for the consciousness that is a seed.' It does not occur to craving, 'I moisten the consciousness that is a seed.' It does not occur to ignorance, 'I sow the consciousness that is a seed.' And it does not occur to the consciousness that is a seed, 'I am produced by these conditions.'

"However, when the consciousness that is a seed, which is supported on the field of karma, watered by the moisture of craving, and planted with the fertilizer of ignorance, germinates, then the sprout of name-and-form is produced in this and that mother's womb, the place of birth, reconnection. And that sprout of name-and-form was not made by itself, not made by another, not made by both, not made by Īśvara, not transformed by time, not arisen from nature, not dependent on an agent, and not born without a cause. Nevertheless, if the mother and father unite, the time is fertile, and the other conditions are gathered, then because the causes and conditions are not deficient in those dharmas without a governor, without [the notion] 'mine,' without grasping, equal to space, and having the essential nature of the mark of illusion, the consciousness that is a seed that relishes in experience will produce the sprout of name-and-form in this and that mother's womb, the place of birth, reconnection.

"In this way, visual consciousness arises through five causes. What are the five? Depending on the eye, form, light, space, and attention produced from that, visual consciousness arises. Regarding that, the eye performs the function of the basis of visual consciousness. Form performs the function of the image for visual consciousness. Light performs the function of illumination. Space performs the function of nonobstruction. Attention produced from that performs the function of taking notice. Without those conditions, visual consciousness will not arise, but when the eye, the internal sense-base, is not deficient, and similarly form, light, space, and attention produced from that are not deficient, from the assemblage of all those, visual consciousness will arise. Regarding that, it does not occur to the eye, 'I perform the function of the basis of visual consciousness.' It does not occur to form, 'I perform the function of image for visual consciousness.' It does not occur to light, 'I perform the function of illumination for visual consciousness.' It does not occur to space, 'I perform the function of nonobstruction for visual consciousness.' It does not occur to attention produced from that, 'I perform the function of "taking notice" for visual consciousness.' And it does not occur to visual consciousness, 'I am produced by these conditions.' Nevertheless, when these conditions are present, visual consciousness will be born. Likewise, this applies as appropriate to the remaining sense organs as well.

"Regarding that, while indeed no dharma at all passes from this world to the next, because causes and conditions are not deficient, the result of karma appears. Thus, for example, though the reflection of a face appears in the orb of a clean mirror while indeed the face is not transferred to the mirror, because the causes and conditions are not deficient, a face appears. Likewise, no one departs from this world and is born in another, but because the causes and conditions are not deficient, the result of karma appears.

"Thus, for example, the orb of the moon wanders 42,000 yojanas above; nevertheless, the reflection of the orb of the moon appears in a small vessel filled with water even though the orb of the moon is not transferred from that place. While indeed the moon does not go inside the small water-filled vessel, because the causes and conditions are not deficient, the orb of the moon appears. Likewise, while indeed no one departs from this world and is born in another, because causes and conditions are not deficient, the result of karma appears.

"Thus, for example, fire does not flame when causes and conditions are deficient, but from causes and conditions gathering, fire flames. Similarly, because causes and conditions are not deficient in those dharmas without a governor, without [the notion] 'mine,' without grasping, equal to space, and having the essential nature of the mark of illusion, a consciousness that is a seed germinated by karma and defilement produces the sprout of name-and-form in this or that mother's womb, the place of birth, reconnection. In that way, the dependence on conditions of internal dependent arising is to be seen.

"Regarding that, internal dependent arising is to be seen as fivefold. What five? Not eternalism, not annihilation, not transmigration, a great result arises from a small cause, and the continuity of what is similar to that.

"How is [internal dependent arising] not eternalism? Because the aggregates of death are one and those partaking of birth are another. Precisely those which are the aggregates of death are not those partaking of birth, but because when the aggregates of death cease, the aggregates partaking of birth arise, therefore [internal dependent arising] is not eternalism.

"How is it not annihilation? The aggregates of birth do not arise from aggregates of death that have already ceased, and the aggregates of birth do not arise from aggregates of death that have not [yet] ceased. But when the aggregates of death cease, at that very moment the aggregates partaking of birth arise like the high and low ends of a balance beam. Thus [internal dependent arising] is not annihilation.

"How is it not transmigration? From different species of beings arises birth in a common species, and therefore [internal dependent arising] is not transmigration.

"How does a great result arise from a small cause? One experiences the ripening of a great result from performing a small karma, so therefore a great result is produced from a small cause.

"Whatever type of karma is performed, the corresponding ripening is experienced, so there is therefore continuity of what is similar to that.

"Reverend Śāriputra, whoever, by means of perfect discriminating insight, sees this dependent arising perfectly taught by the Blessed One accordingly—in reality, continuous in perpetuity, without life, free of life, just as it is, unerring, unborn, unarisen, not made, unconditioned, unobstructed, baseless, peaceful, fearless, not to be taken away, not exhausted, as an essential nature that is not pacified—and regards it as nonexistent, trifling, hollow, without essence, diseased, infected, a thorn, evil, impermanent, suffering, empty, and selfless, he does not reflect upon the past: Did I exist in the past or did I not exist in the past? What was I in the past? How was I in the past? He does not reflect upon the future: Will I exist in the future or not exist in the future? In the future what will I become? In the future how will I exist? Similarly, he does not reflect upon the present: What is this? How is this? What is there? What will this become? From where has this being come? Having departed [from this world], where will it go?

"In the world, whatever different [philosophical] views of ascetics and brāhmaṇas there are, namely: belief in the self, belief in a life force, belief in a person, belief in the festive and salutary, excessive movement and lack of movement; those [views] that, at that time, have been eliminated, comprehended, and uprooted by that one, like the top of the palm tree that does not later appear, [they] are dharmas that do not arise or cease.

"Reverend Śāriputra, if someone possessing such forbearance for the Dharma correctly understands this dependent arising, for that one the Tathāgata, Arhat, Complete Buddha, the One Endowed with Knowledge and Good Conduct, Sugata, Knower of the World, Captain Who Disciplines

Beings, the Unsurpassed, the Teacher of Gods and Humans, Buddha, the Blessed One will predict the unsurpassed perfectly complete enlightenment saying, '[You] will become a perfectly complete buddha.'"

The bodhisattva great being Maitreya, having spoken thus, the Venerable Śāriputra and the world of humans, gods, asuras, and gandharvas, rejoicing, praised the explanation by the bodhisattva great being Maitreya.

The noble Mahayana sutra entitled *The Rice Seedling* is completed.

1. How to Seek Reality by Means of Buddha's Teaching on Dependent Arising

——— ◆ ———

The Sage, the Buddha, is regarded as the unsurpassed teacher or guru of all beings because he understood and taught the way of dependent arising through his own direct experience. The Buddha perceived that all living beings are afflicted with a variety of problems because, as an initial cause, they misconceive the way things are. Motivated by the wish to show precisely the ontological status of all things in order to completely free all beings from these problems, the Teacher—the Buddha—revealed the truth of dependent arising.

The main cause of all the troubles in the world is our ignorance. This is twofold. First, we do not precisely understand the dependent arising of causes and effects—in other words, how effects depend on their respective causes for their production. Second, we do not think about how things derive their respective identities and become an object of the mind merely by our imputing a term or concept onto their parts—their so-called basis of imputation. We think instead that if we searched for what they truly are, we would be able to find them. For instance, we each have an ever-present and instinctual notion of "I" and "mine" to which a self appears to exist in its own right and that assents to this appearance. Based on this, we conceive things in two groups: (1) anything associated with ourselves—"myself," "mine," "my family," "my race," "my country," "my religion," and so on—and (2) anything associated with others—that is to say, everything else. We then have attachment for the former and hostility for the latter, and all our other problems ensue.

If you reflect deeply on dependent arising, you will understand that whatever identity things have is established in dependence on a collection of causes and conditions as well as on a basis of imputation and imputing terms and concepts. With this key point, you see that things such as "self" and "other" are established merely by conceptualization, and from this you can easily understand that they lack intrinsic existence. The mere fact that things arise dependently induces certain knowledge that all actions and their agents can function even though they lack intrinsic existence. The knowledge that things are empty of intrinsic existence overcomes the eternalistic view that things have intrinsic existence. The knowledge that things are able to perform functions despite lacking intrinsic existence automatically destroys the nihilistic view that things lacking intrinsic existence cannot perform functions.

Furthermore, those who believe they are inherently superior or inherently inferior to others, who are attached to an intrinsic notion of themselves as high status or low status, experience trouble in this life and will experience trouble in lives to come. Those who think that their high or low status or their particular occupation is a dependent arising, in either a coarse or subtle sense, and in accordance with this understanding, make timely effort to adopt what needs to be done and cast aside what needs to be abandoned will easily achieve happiness and well-being in this and future lives.

Thus the Teacher explained to his disciples that the mind of a supreme deity could not create the helpful or harmful things that are the basis of our joy or sorrow. He also taught that such things are not produced causelessly, from a principal nature, or from a permanent entity called "time."[4] Rather, he said, they arise dependently, based on their respective causes and conditions. This teaching eliminates any misconception of how things are produced and illuminates how they actually are. Accordingly, it is principally up to you yourself to clear away the suffering that you do not want and to achieve the happiness that you do want. The teaching of dependent arising is the Buddha's unsurpassed act of skillful means to help you understand what you should do in order to eliminate suffering and achieve happiness.

All things arise in dependence on their respective causes and conditions; they do not arise without a cause. And not just any cause can produce any effect. Rather, when the causes and conditions endowed with the specific and particular potential for producing each phenomenon come together and undergo a sequential transformation, the effect arises. Thus the products of both the animate and inanimate worlds need not arise in dependence on the expressed will or thought of a divine creator, such as Īśvara, who thinks, "I will cause this to arise."

Furthermore, effects are not caused by a permanent entity called "time," a permanent partless particle, or a single indivisible cause. All causes and conditions are composite—they invariably have parts—and none of these causes and conditions can produce an effect without themselves undergoing transformation. No cause reaches its resultant state or is somehow transferred to its resultant state without undergoing some change. Moreover, it is not the case that the causes and conditions cease and then the effects somehow arise; nor is it the case that the continuum of the causes ceases and thereafter the effects arise. Instead, the cessation of the causes and the production of the effects are simultaneous and connected without any cessation of the continuum. It is just like the two sides of a scale, where when the one side goes down the other side simultaneously goes up.

Therefore, when the Blessed One spoke the term "dependent and linked arising" (for which *dependent arising* is a contraction), he was using "dependent," or "dependent on causes and conditions," to refute the view of objects being produced causelessly and being established independently. He was using "linked" to refute the view that things arise from a discordant cause—an enduring, changeless cause. He was using "arising" to show that effects are not completely nonexistent, nor are they independently established; rather, they fully arise from their own causes and conditions, dependently. Consequently, the Blessed One used the convention "dependent and linked arising" with respect to things for two purposes: (1) to end the misconception that composite things exist from their own side, independently, and to end thereby the faults that ensue from this misconception, and (2) to show that with respect to all dependently arisen phenomena, all presentations of actions and agents are coherent in being mere dependent imputations.

THE DEFINITION OF THE DEPENDENT
ARISING OF COMPOSITE PHENOMENA

The *Rice Seedling Sutra* says:

> Because this exists, this occurs; because this arose, this arises; this is called *dependent arising*. That is, dependent on ignorance, conditioning factors occur . . .

Thus all composite things have causes, and effects do not exist at the time of their causes. Therefore effects are not the same entity as their causes.

"Because this [causes and conditions] exists, this [effects] occurs" means that composite things do not arise from a divine creator, such as Īśvara, thinking, "I will produce this." Rather, when these causes and conditions (which are concordant with the effects they produce) exist—that is, when a variety of causes and conditions exist—a variety of new effects (which are composite things) will certainly arise. Thus these new effects arise from causes that are not a divine creator's thought.

Also, when these effects that are composite things are produced, they do not come from causes and conditions that are unitary, partless, or permanent in the sense of being unchanging—in other words, any discordant causes such as partless particles and so on. The sutra states that because the specific and ever-changing causes and conditions of the effects were produced, they will produce these effects: "because this arose, this arises." Accordingly, effects arise from many causes that are impermanent and have parts.

Moreover, a composite thing does not arise from a permanent cause, as this would not have the capacity to give rise to it. It is not the case that just any cause with the capacity to generate an effect gives rise to just any effect. Rather, a specific cause—one with a capacity that corresponds to the effect that it will produce—gives rise to the effect. Thus the sutra states, "dependent on ignorance, conditioning factors occur," indicating that composite things arise from causes that have the capacity to produce them.[5]

In short, composite things are produced from their specific existent causes and conditions. If these specific causes and conditions do not exist, then these composite phenomena are not produced. Therefore the citation from sutra above affirms with certainty that effects are produced from causes that have a direct relationship with their effects in that the effects ensue once the causes exist and do not arise when the causes are absent.

In the *Sutra Explaining the First Factor of Dependent Arising and Its Divisions* and other sutras on dependent arising, the question arises, "What is dependent arising?" This question asks, what are the causes and conditions of external and internal things, and how do they produce the composite things that are their effects? As he did in the *Rice Seedling Sutra* above, the Buddha responds:

Because this exists, this occurs; because this arose, this arises; this is called *dependent arising*. That is, dependent on ignorance, conditioning factors occur . . .[6]

The Buddha implies that the definition of the dependent arising of composite phenomena is production through the three causes: (1) production from a cause that is not a divine creator's thoughts, (2) production from [multiple] impermanent causes, and (3) production from a cause that has the capacity to give rise to the effect.

Again, in the *Sutra Enumerating Phenomena Called "Discerning the Divisions of Existence and the Rest,"* the Buddha, in response to a question regarding the definition of *dependent arising*, elaborates on production from the three causes:

> O monks! There are three defining characteristics of dependent arising: (1) production from a cause that is not a divine creator's thoughts, (2) production from [multiple] impermanent causes, and (3) production from a cause that has the capacity to give rise to the effect.[7]

The *Rice Seedling Sutra* adds two more to this list—production from existing causes and production from selfless causes—thereby giving a clear and detailed explanation of both internal and external dependent arisings from the viewpoint of all five defining characteristics.

In his *Verses on the Rice Seedling Sutra*, Nāgārjuna says:

> Nothing is produced from itself or from other,
> from both, or from "time,"
> from a divine creator, such as Īśvara,
> from a principal nature, or without a cause.

> An arising from causes and conditions
> comes from beginningless time;
> thus you assert that external things arise
> in dependence on the five causes.[8]

Also, Nāgārjuna says in his *Extensive Commentary on the Rice Seedling Sutra*:

> Aside from seeds and so forth
> there are no other causes;
> Īśvara and causelessness
> contradict the obvious and so on.[9]

As a commentary to this verse he says, "Seeds and so forth produce sprouts and so forth. Īśvara, the principal nature, time, and the like are not the causes of sprouts, for these causes would be just like flowers growing in the sky: not perceived either by direct perception or by inference."

DEPENDENT ARISING OF COMPOSITE PHENOMENA

The *Rice Seedling Sutra* explains the dependent arising of a composite phenomenon by using a rice seedling as an illustration. If a rice seedling were produced without any causes or conditions, it would have to be produced constantly in all places or it would never be produced anywhere at any time. Instead, it is sometimes produced and sometimes not produced, so we can establish that it has causes and conditions.

Some might assert, as did some Indian philosophers, that the seedling already exists at the time of its causes and conditions and that it is simply not yet manifest. But if the seedling had already been produced and existed at that time, it would then be unnecessary for it to be produced yet again by its causes and conditions. Furthermore, if we postulate that the seedling's causal continuum is somehow broken and that it is produced from something other than its causal continuum, the effect (the seedling) would have to be independent of its causes. As it would be produced without any relationship to its causes and conditions, anything would be able to produce it.

Nothing that is indivisibly unitary, unchangeably permanent, and substantially independent can give rise to an effect. Thus causes with such characteristics cannot produce a rice seedling. Instead, the seedling must be produced from a cause that is a composite thing, is dependently arisen, has multiple parts, and changes every moment. Therefore, as we will investigate in more detail in the next chapter, there can be no master of the world, no divine creator who creates the world merely by thinking it. The world is definitely created from causes and conditions.

An assemblage of causes and conditions such as a seed, water, fertilizer, warmth, and moisture produces the seedling. This assemblage carries a capacity that corresponds with the production of its effect and is connected to the effect—the seedling—through a gradual transformation, moment by moment. It is impossible for this seedling to arise from a cause that does not itself undergo momentary change or without this process of change contributing to the production of the effect.

A cause has the quality of producing the entity of its effect; in other words, it has the property of reaching its effect. The only way for a cause to produce its effect is through a gradual process of transformation of the cause. Given that an effect cannot occur without some aspect of the cause undergoing transformation, there can be no cause that becomes its effect directly. Nevertheless, it is not the case that an effect occurs only after the cause has completely ceased to exist, such that the continuum of the cause has been cut. It is instead like the two sides of a scale, where when the one side goes down, the other side simultaneously goes up; when the cause ceases to exist, the effect occurs simultaneously. Therefore the effect arises in a way that is linked to the cause.

In this manner, a seedling does not exist at the time of its causes and conditions; that is to say, it does not exist simultaneously with its cause. Moreover, it does not come from somewhere else later on. A seedling is a dependent arising that appears and disappears like a magician's illusion: it arises suddenly, composed from causes at a certain point in the continuum of momentary transformations of its causes, and when it ceases to exist, it does not go somewhere else.

It is impossible for any effect or cause to be established independently. All transformations within a continuum do not arise and cease on their own but do so by the power of their specific causes and conditions. In the collection of causes and conditions there is a constant change or flux; they are never static. The effect arises in a way that is linked or connected to the constantly changing continuum of causes. This is then aptly called "the dependent and linked arising of composite phenomena."

In the same manner, a rice seedling is not produced in isolation but from the transformation that is the dependent arising of its causes and conditions; no independent divine creator or master of the universe is involved. A rice seedling is momentary in the sense that the rice seedling of the first moment has ceased to exist in the second moment of the rice seedling. So the second moment of a rice seedling did not exist previously. It was produced newly and adventitiously from its causes and conditions—that is, from both the preceding moment that is part of a continuum of rice seedling moments that are of similar type and conditions such as warmth, moisture, and air. It is not the case that a portion of the rice seedling's continuum that has already been produced lingers on.

Therefore all external and internal composite things—rice seedlings, people, thoughts—are produced in dependence on an aggregation of their multiple and varied causes and conditions, which are specific to each thing, composed of parts, and ever changing. When these things are produced, it is impossible for them to be produced as singular partless things. Since any effect is produced only from an assemblage of multiple and varied parts, it is impossible for it to come into being without depending or relying on a collection of parts, which is its basis of imputation.

DIFFERENT INTERPRETATIONS OF
HOW AN EFFECT DEPENDS ON ITS CAUSES

Since even essentialists—those who say that the identity of individual phenomena relies on their possessing a fixed essence or nature—assert that effects arise in dependence on their causes, they must ultimately deny any mode of existence that is independent of causes and conditions, just as consequentialists do.[10] Therefore one may wonder how consequentialists differ from essentialists with respect to their understanding of the dependent arising of composite phenomena. Different essentialists make various assertions with regard to composite phenomena. Some say that things arise causelessly, whereas others assert various discordant causes, such as a divine creator, a partless particle, a permanent principle called "time," a principal nature, or a permanent being. These various positions can be subsumed within four alternatives: (1) production from self—effects arise from causes that are the same nature as themselves, (2) production from other—effects arise from causes that exist in and of themselves, (3) production from both self and other, and (4) production from no cause (i.e., causeless production). Thus they assert production from one of these four.

That the production of effects via these four alternatives is unfeasible has already been explained above. Therefore, although essentialists say that effects arise in dependence on their causes, they do not in fact assert how effects do arise—how they arise from causes that are concordant with them.

Unlike essentialists, consequentialists do not assert that all effects—sprouts or anything else—arise from causes such as the above-mentioned four alternatives. Rather, they assert that an effect arises newly and suddenly from a stream of its specific, ever-changing causes to which it is linked. Candrakīrti states in his *Entering the Middle Way* (6.114):

> Composite phenomena
> do not arise causelessly,
> from a cause such as a divine creator,
> or from both themselves and others;
> they arise dependently.

The General Meaning of Dependent Arising

Consequentialists do not qualify only composite phenomena as dependently arisen. Rather, they describe all phenomena—composite and noncomposite—as dependent arisings. Noncomposite phenomena are things like space (in the sense of a mere lack of obstructive contact). In this broad meaning of dependent arising, *dependent* does not mean only dependent on the causes and conditions that give rise to the effects but also dependent on a basis of imputation—its parts and so forth—and dependent on the conventional terms and concepts that are the tools of imputation. It also refers to the mutual dependence of such causally unconnected things as the near hill and the far hill, or short and long. The word *arising* not only means production (from causes and conditions) but is also understood as "existence" or "establishment." Therefore, from the viewpoint of this broader sense of the term *dependent arising*, consequentialists assert that all phenomena—composite and noncomposite—are dependent arisings. As Nāgārjuna states in his *Fundamental Verses on the Middle Way* (24.19):

Since there is no phenomenon
that is not dependently arisen,
there is no phenomenon
that is not empty.

Thus the term *dependent arising* applies to all phenomena because all phenomena are dependent on their basis of imputation—their parts and so forth—and then are established as an object of the mind in relation to that basis of imputation and in dependence on imputing terms and concepts. In other words, it refers to phenomena being dependent on their parts and so forth, being apprehended as the basis of imputation, and then being established in dependence on imputation by terms and concepts.

For instance, the establishment or existence of a carriage is completed when you identify its parts (the wheels, chassis, and so on), which are apprehended as the basis of imputation, and then conceptually impute to them the conventional designation "carriage." Therefore a carriage is established in dependence both on its parts and on imputing terms and concepts.

Likewise, with respect to the example of the Buddha's cousin Devadatta walking on the road, his walking is established by merely imputing, "Devadatta is walking on the road" in dependence on Devadatta, the road, the lifting up and placing down of his feet, and so on. Other than this establishment of Devadatta's walking in dependence on the basis of imputation and the imputing terms and concepts, where is there an independent action of Devadatta walking? If there were such an independent action of walking, then its ontological status would not be encompassed by merely imputing "Devadatta is walking on the road"; it would necessarily exist in its own right. Were this the case, then when you searched among the bases of imputation, you should find it and should be able to say, "Here is the action of walking." In this manner, the *Fundamental Verses on the Middle Way* refutes this findability after it analyzes whether this walking exists in the road, in the movement of the feet, and so on.

ANOTHER WAY OF ESTABLISHING DEPENDENCE

Devadatta being a doer of an action is established in dependence on the action he performs. The action also is established in dependence on the doer. Aside from this, there is no way to establish the doer or the action as essentially existent. The *Fundamental Verses on the Middle Way* (8.12) says:

> The doer depends on the action,
> the action is dependent on the doer;
> except for arising dependently,
> there is no other way they are established.

Likewise, Madhyamaka texts such as the *Fundamental Verses* refute essential existence with respect to parts and wholes, objects of cognition and valid cognitions, producers and products, and so on. They then reveal these things to be dependent arisings that are posited as interdependent or mutually dependent. For instance, dependent on the far hill we posit the near hill, and dependent on the near hill we posit the far hill. They exist interdependently but do not exist otherwise as such. It is the same with east and west, self and other, and so forth.

To establish such things as fire and smoke to be cause and effect is also done on the basis of their being mutually dependent. The fire's nature being hot and burning and its being the cause of smoke is established in dependence on the fuel and smoke, respectively, just as firewood is established in dependence on fire. Therefore, the consequentialist Prāsaṅgikas assert that not only is the effect dependent on its cause but the cause is also established in dependence on its effect. Candrakīrti's *Clear Words* commentary on Nāgārjuna's text states:

> Therefore the four valid cognitions establish knowledge of the world's objects.[11] They too are interdependently established. Once valid cognitions exist, they have their objects of cognition; and once objects of cognition exist, they have their valid cognitions. Both valid cognitions and objects of cognition are not established by their own intrinsic essence.[12]

Buddhapālita's commentary says:

> It is like this: due to interdependence, there is fire in dependence on firewood, and there is firewood in dependence on fire.[13]

Nāgārjuna's *Precious Garland* (1.48) says:

> When this is, that arises,
> like short when there is long.
> Due to the production of this, that is produced,
> like light from the production of a flame.

The *Verse Summary Sutra* states:

> Air depends on space, and the body of water depends on this air;
>   the great earth depends on this water, and beings depend on the
>   great earth.
> In this way beings experience their karma.
> Consider: How else would space serve as a base for something?[14]

The master Haribhadra's *Commentary on the Verse Summary Sutra* explains:

> The verse states "on space" and so forth. For example, this uni-
> verse evolves in stages that are dependent on each other. Air
> depends on space, the body of water depends on air, the golden
> earth depends on the body of water, the great earth depends on
> the golden earth, and the world system comprised of the four
> continents is dependent on the great earth. Then the resources
> of living beings form. Consider how karma is the root cause of
> this. How else could space—defined as the absence of all
> things—serve as the base? What need is there to mention every-
> thing for which air is the basis?[15]

Thus this world's environment and the beings that use its resources have
all been interdependent and interconnected right from the beginning of
this world. At the present moment, too, the fact that all beings—humans
and so on—are alive is dependent on the external and internal elements—
earth, water, fire, air, empty space, and so forth.

The living beings that inhabit this world are dependent on this world's
environment. The great earth that is part of this world's environment
depends on the body of water, which in turn depends on the great mass of
air. This air depends on empty space. This empty space—the mere absence

of all things—serves as the basis for the things that cause beings to experience happiness and suffering: their bodies, the earth and its resources, and so on. The period of time that it remains as such is dependent on these beings' karma. If this were not true, the empty space of the present could not become a suitable basis for air and so on. Thus the citation states that beings' karma is the root cause of the world's environment and its inhabitants.

Hence dependent arising is taught in two sets of two: (1) the dependent arising of dependence on something else to establish something's identity (e.g., far and near, cognition and its object) and the dependent arising of dependence on something else's attributes (e.g., good and bad); and (2) the dependent arising of dependent imputation (e.g., an object of imputation and its basis) and the dependent arising of dependent production (e.g., effects and their causes).

How Phenomena Are Established in Dependence on Their Basis of Imputation

The rice seedling is produced just from an aggregation of a variety of factors, composite causes and conditions that are constantly undergoing change—its seed, the four great elements, the element of empty space, and so on. When the rice seedling is produced, it is produced not as one singular thing but only as an aggregation of various things. The individual parts and the aggregation are not the rice seedling, and there is no entity other than these parts that is the rice seedling. When we nonetheless say, "This is a rice seedling," we are imputing a conventional term on a basis of imputation that consists of different parts, such as the upper and lower halves, the color, and so on. This mere imputation of "rice seedling" encompasses the ontological status of the rice seedling. Not content with just this, however, we search for that which is the rice seedling, the object of the imputation "rice seedling." When we do, we find no rice seedling that is the parts—the bases of imputation—or something other than the parts. Therefore this rice seedling is a dependent arising that is established in dependence on its parts and imputing terms and concepts.

If any one part of the basis of imputation were found to be the rice seedling itself, it would be incorrect to assert that the rice seedling arises in dependence on the basis of imputation and the imputing terms and concepts. However, none of the parts can be found to be the rice seedling, and yet the rice seedling does exist by mere imputation of "rice seedling," by imputing the term and concept to the basis of imputation, its parts. Therefore the rice seedling exists in dependence on its parts and its imputing terms and concepts. We cannot identify the rice seedling as existing without depending on its parts and imputing terms and concepts, so we establish the rice seedling to be a dependent arising.

Just as the rice seedling is established in this way in dependence on its parts, the individual parts themselves—the upper and lower portions, the color, and so on—are established in dependence on their basis of imputation—their parts—and the imputing terms and concepts. If, after dividing parts into parts in this way, you arrive at some microscopic particle, this particle, providing it has an identity, will certainly have multiple sides, such as east and west, and depend on many other particles. For this reason, consequentialists assert that it is impossible to have a partless, indivisible, solitary particle. Why is this so? As long as something is a particle, it must be established by way of its imputing terms and concepts and the many parts that are its basis of imputation. So in a consequentialist system, the impossibility of a partless particle establishes all particles to be dependent arisings.

The Unfindability of the Imputed Object

From the beginning, you need to understand the following. When the different Buddhist philosophical schools speak of something being established dependently or of something not being established independently, they are using similar terminology. However, they differ in the extent of the dependence and the range of independence they assert, with some views being more coarse and other views being more subtle. Therefore, when they similarly use the expression "empty of being established independently," their positions range from gross to subtle.

For example, for essentialists the fact that a rice seedling is produced in dependence on its causes and conditions is enough grounds to claim that, on analysis, it must be found to exist independently, intrinsically, from its own side, and in its own right. The position of consequentialists is quite the opposite. They state that a rice seedling gains its identity in dependence on the constant change of a great variety of causes and conditions, and that this seedling—the result—has numerous parts. The rice seedling is fully established merely through its being imputed, "This is a rice seedling," by term and concept in dependence on these parts—its colors, shape, upper and lower parts, and so forth. It is only when you are still not satisfied with this, and you look further for that which is this rice seedling—this imputed object—that you never find it either in the individual parts of the seedling or in the collection of these parts. Thus consequentialists assert that not even the slightest particle is independently established, intrinsically established, and so forth.

For the Buddhist essentialists, the schools other than the Prāsaṅgikas, sutras like the *Rice Seedling Sutra* are able to refute some gross levels of independence, such as independence in the sense of being permanent (that is, not dependent on causes and conditions), but they insist that the way a rice seedling exists cannot be fully established through merely being designated "rice seedling." The object imputed as "seedling" must be findable to be the objectively existent object imputed, such that you say, "This is it." The consequentialist Prāsaṅgikas, however, assert that a rice seedling is not an object that exists objectively; rather, they posit that it exists in dependence on its parts and in dependence on the conventions that are the imputing names and concepts. Thus only in the Prāsaṅgika school do they know how to set forth the concept of the subtle dependent arising that repudiates the notion of the objective existence of an object; none of the other schools of tenets know how to do this.

How Dependent Arising Refutes the Object of Negation

Therefore the existence of any object is fully established by merely being designated as such and such by its imputing conventions—terms and concepts—in dependence on your mind having apprehended its parts and so forth to be its basis of imputation. Anything not established in this manner, then, would be posited to exist independently or to exist by way of its intrinsic essence. Thus Candrakīrti's *Commentary on the Four Hundred Stanzas* states:

> *Self* [in the term *selflessness*] refers to the intrinsic nature or essence of things that is independent of anything else. The lack of this kind of self is selflessness. Based on the division [of the

basis of selflessness] into persons and objects (*dharmas*), there is the selflessness of persons and selflessness of objects.[16]

It would not be feasible for anything with independent existence to possess multiple parts or to exist in dependence on its parts and its imputing terms and concepts. To exist in dependence on something else requires having parts. To put this another way, were a sprout, for example, to exist independently, with an essence that you could find, then it would have to exist only in isolation, without depending on causes and conditions, and would not be identified as an aggregation of the elements and so forth that serve as its basis of imputation. However, this is not the case. Instead, forms such as seedlings exist as entities that are an aggregation of the eight substances.[17] In the absence of those substances they would no longer exist. Therefore objects exist dependently and cannot exist objectively from their own side.

If a thing were partless, it would be untenable for it to exist dependently or conventionally. Once an individual phenomenon exists dependently and conventionally, it is tenable for it to have parts and have a nature that is manifold. Therefore something being a dependent arising refutes its having an independent or objective existence. This reasoning is profound and subtle and the ultimate reason for this kind of refutation.

The Buddha was considering the above-mentioned way that a rice seedling is produced [from causes and conditions] and exists [by way of depending on its basis of imputation and imputing terms and concepts] when he looked at a rice seedling and told his monks that whoever understands the dependent arising of a rice seedling understands the ontological status of the Buddha Jewel and the Dharma Jewel. The Buddha did not invent the way of dependent arising and the way of emptiness. Rather, he just clearly taught—through his own power, without others—what in fact exists, for whether buddhas appear in the world or not, the dependent arising of phenomena (their conventional reality) and their lack of objective existence (their ultimate reality) remain unchanged.

How to Seek the View

An unmistaken exposition of the path and its resultant states depends on how you ascertain the philosophical view of phenomena. The method of ascertaining this view must be able to determine that dependent arising and emptiness complement one another. Essentialists see them as contradictory, like hot and cold. As long as they do not see emptiness as the meaning of dependent arising, they cannot free themselves from falling into either the extreme of eternalism or the extreme of nihilism.

However, in the system of the consequentialist Prāsaṅgika scholars, when you ascertain these two, not only do dependent arising and emptiness not contradict each other, but also the understanding of one serves to enhance the understanding of the other. It is because the rice seedling exists dependently that it is empty of existing in its own right, independently. Moreover, it is because it is empty of existing in its own right that it exists dependently. This combination of appearance and emptiness—wherein dependent arising is the meaning of emptiness and emptiness is the meaning of dependent arising—is illusion-like existence, or the middle way that is free of the two extremes. This is the sacred key point in how to posit dependent arising that is unique to the Madhyamaka Prāsaṅgika school. With this in mind, Nāgārjuna states in his *Dispelling Debates*:

> I bow down to the unparalleled Buddha,
> who made the most excellent statement
> that *emptiness* and *dependent arising*
> have the same meaning as the *middle path*.[18]

Emptiness in this context does not mean that composite phenomena lack the ability to perform functions. Rather, *emptiness* here means to be empty of intrinsic or independent existence. Candrakīrti's *Clear Words* states:

> We are not saying that action, agent, and effect do not exist. What do we mean? We posit that these phenomena have no intrinsic nature.[19]

Qualm: Well then, it is not feasible for things with no intrinsic nature to perform functions, and you are still subject to the same fault mentioned above.

Answer: That is not true. It is only things that possess intrinsic nature that cannot function. It is only things that *lack* intrinsic existence that can function.

Although everything is empty of independent existence, the functioning of causality is feasible within mere dependent existence. This is extremely difficult to understand and is also said to be the most profound and cherished principle in the treasury of the Tathāgata's teachings. Nāgārjuna's *Fundamental Verses on the Middle Way* (24.12) states:

> Because he understood that his teaching
> would be difficult for others to fathom,
> the Buddha decided
> not to share it with others.

Nāgārjuna's *Friendly Letter*:

> This dependent arising is what is profound and cherished
> in the treasury of the Conqueror's teachings.[20]

Thus, when you seek the middle path, you must take an object such as a rice seedling and search for this path in terms of the presentation of (1) the dependent arising of the causality involved in both its creation and destruction and (2) the dependent arising involved in its being imputed on a basis of imputation. *Fundamental Verses on the Middle Way* (24.18) states:

> Whatever is dependently arisen,
> that is explained to be emptiness.
> That, being a dependent imputation,
> is itself the middle way.

The *Rice Seedling Sutra*:

> The Blessed One, after looking at a rice seedling, spoke this sutra to the monks: "Monks, whoever sees dependent arising sees the Dharma; whoever sees the Dharma sees the Buddha."

Therefore you should not accept the statement, "dependently arisen phenomena lack an intrinsic nature" merely because it is the Buddha's wish or because the Buddha has some power, as you would accept the edict of a king. Rather, there are limitless reasons establishing this statement to be true. Among these, the ultimate and peerless reason that proves this lack of being established by an intrinsic nature is the reason of dependent arising. Indian and Tibetan scholars praised this reason of dependent arising, saying, "the reason of dependent arising is the king of reasons." This is a key point that should be contemplated again and again.

The Contradiction in One Thing Being Both the Basis of Imputation and the Object Imputed

The *person*, or *self*, in connection with a human being arises from a collection of various causes and conditions that are collections of perishing objects. There is nothing that is the self from among the bases of imputation of "self"—the organs, the senses, and the five psychophysical aggregates (*skandhas*). There is also nothing that is the self that is a separate entity from these bases of imputation. Thus the self, which is nevertheless able to function, is posited by merely imputing the convention "self" in dependence on the aggregates and so forth.

The treatises often compare the self to a chariot. Just as none of the bases of imputation of a chariot—its parts—are suitable to *be* the chariot, so none of the bases of imputation of the self—the aggregates and so forth—are suitable to be the self, the reason being that the "self" is imputed in dependence on the aggregates and the rest. Therefore it is said that it is not feasible for the basis of imputation—that in dependence on which something else is imputed—to be the imputed thing. Candrakīrti's *Entering the Middle Way* states (6.135cd):

> The sutra states that [the self] is [imputed] in dependence on
> the aggregates.
> Therefore the mere combination of the aggregates is not the self.

Thus, whether you use the word *self* or *person*, it exists simply as a dependent arising, existing in dependence on causes and conditions and the aggregates and so forth that are its bases of imputation. There is no way to find something that is the self from among the aggregates. Nor can you find some entity that is separate from the aggregates that serve as its basis of imputation. If there *were* a findable self, it would have to be a self that was independent or that existed by its own intrinsic nature. However, it is impossible to find something that is the self after searching in this way. In this vein, Nāgārjuna's *Precious Garland* (1.80) states:

> The person is not earth, not water,
> not fire, not wind, not space,
> not consciousness, not all of these.
> Yet what person is there apart from these?

With Dependent Arising, Both Bondage and Liberation Are Possible

Due to karma and the afflictions, the five aggregates—form, feeling, discrimination, compositional factors, and consciousness—continually change each instant without any independence and are therefore known as "the source of bother," "that which brings suffering," and "cyclic existence." These aggregates have no independence; produced and destroyed due to karma and the afflictions, they are constantly in flux across a stream of moments, wherein the aggregates of the present moment are of a similar type to the aggregates of the former moment. On certain occasions, when there is a coarse change, you use the conventional terms "birth" and "death." As long as a person must be connected to and dependent on such a stream of momentarily changing aggregates, this person is posited as someone "belonging to cyclic existence."

Nevertheless, it is not necessary for the person to always remain this way. In general, from the viewpoint of this stream of change, both consciousness and the person transform from one situation to another either in terms of the causes and conditions on which they depend or in terms of their bases of imputation. Within the framework of dependent arising, it is quite possible that bad situations can become good and good situations can become bad. Therefore, if those who desire liberation make strong effort, they can gradually reduce the karma contaminated by ignorance and gradually increase both wisdom and method—the wisdom that precisely knows the ontological status of things and the method of making effort at the imperative to help all living beings and to provide them all with happiness. With dependent arising, it is certainly possible for your consciousness to become free of all decline, to become completely free of all trouble, and to reach buddhahood.

2. Analysis of the Divine Creator

INVESTIGATING WHAT KIND OF DIVINE CREATOR WOULD EXIST OR NOT EXIST

In the second section of the previous chapter, I gave citations regarding composite phenomena having the characteristics of arising dependently from either three or five conditions. Among these conditions was the condition of arising not from the thought of a creator god. In this chapter, we will look more closely at this arising from the condition of a lack of a divine creator's will, relying especially on the summary of the reality of dependent arising found in Śāntarakṣita's *Compendium of Reality*. This work begins by praising the Buddha:

> Free from the mass of all elaborations—
> a condition not known by others—
> and not dependent on hearing the Self-Existent Words[21]
> but motivated by the intention to benefit all beings,
>
> the one who has a nature of great compassion,
> not for a short time but for innumerable eons,
> spoke dependent arising
> and became the supreme speaker.
>
> I bow down to this omniscient being
> and will now summarize and explain some truths.[22]

The *Compendium of Reality* elsewhere states:

Lacking a divine creator's will is freedom from creation
by a permanent self, Brahmā, and so forth
and is freedom from creation by the principal nature or by both
this nature and the divine creator.[23]

The non-Buddhists say that what creates internal and external things that arise dependently is either the universal principle that is the principal nature, both this nature and the divine creator, a permanent self, or Brahmā. Many non-Indian religions also posit a creator God. Nevertheless, the Teacher, Buddha, directly saw how things actually are: free of the way non-Buddhists elaborated, using mistaken concepts, that which is dependently arisen.

Qualm: You say, "The Teacher saw the reality of dependent arising." But we non-Buddhists say, for instance:

What is beyond the senses
cannot be directly known.
There is no way of knowing this
other than by the Self-Existent Words.[24]

Is what we say true?

Answer: It is not true. The Buddha saw the truth of dependent arising in the following manner: without being dependent on or connected to hearing the Self-Existent Words—that is, the Vedas or other such scriptures—which are said to be valid by their own nature, he saw this truth on his own and taught it through his direct understanding.

Question: How did the Teacher express his teachings on dependent arising?

Answer: The *Rice Seedling Sutra* states:

The sprout is not made by itself, not made by others, not made by
both, not made by Īśvara, not transformed by time, not arisen from
an essential nature, nor born without a cause. However, the elements
of earth, water, fire, air, space, and season having assembled, when
the seed ceases, the sprout will be produced. Like that, dependence
on conditions of external dependent arising is to be seen.

Once the individual causes and conditions of composite things have assembled, they cease to exist, and the composite thing that is their effect is produced. Therefore this is "dependent and linked arising" or "dependent and precisely correct arising." Things are not able to arise from a lack of causes and conditions or from only one cause. Nor can they arise from a cause that is permanent, changeless, or a singular and partless whole. They each arise from causes that have the capacity to produce them. They cannot be produced by being empowered with the will of a divine creator of the world such as Īśvara.

Qualm: The Blessed One eliminated attachment, hostility, and ignorance and brought his own aims to perfection. Why did he teach the truth of dependent arising so often?

Reply: The *Collection of Aphorisms* states (12.8):

> I taught all of you the path
> that eliminates the suffering of existence.
> The Tathāgata gives teachings;
> you must put them into action.

The Teacher had the purpose neither to benefit or not benefit himself nor to attain or eliminate something for himself. Rather, he long ago acquired a compassionate nature for all beings. Out of this compassion, he intended to clear away all beings' misconceptions of what to adopt and what to discard. Therefore he taught dependent arising. His providing this help also served a purpose: many people who desired freedom from the fear of the miserable rebirths and cyclic existence and many intelligent people intent on higher birth and definite goodness had gone for refuge to the Blessed One. The Teacher needed to protect these beings. That which brings about this protection is ending states of mind that are mistaken as to the causes of beings, their environment, and so forth, generating unmistaken states of mind. These correct states of mind are: precisely knowing the connection between virtuous and nonvirtuous karmic actions and their effects of happiness and suffering, and then having conviction in that connection, as well as knowing the self-lessness of persons and objects. This necessarily arises gradually from study, reflection, and meditation on the Teacher's scriptures, which reveal the unmistaken truth of dependent arising.

Moreover, a sutra states:

> The Blessed One said, "O monks, it is the case that both karma and effects exist. We only impute terms to phenomena. No agent

that discards these aggregates and then appropriates other aggregates can be seen. The phrase 'imputing terms to phenomena' means that once this exists, this arises . . . "[25]

Relying on the method of both compassion and correct knowledge, the Teacher explained to his disciples the truth of dependent arising through his own power, without relying on others. Therefore the Blessed One is a genuine teacher—a refuge for those intent on freedom—and is the excellent and supreme speaker.

PROOF PRESENTED BY OTHER TRADITIONS FOR THE EXISTENCE OF A DIVINE CREATOR

Other traditions that assert the existence of a divine creator of the world say: "You might have assembled the conditions for making a clay pot—a pile of clay, a mallet, and a measuring string—but the pot will not create itself. It needs a conscious entity—the potter. Likewise, although all the causes of a body, a place, and so on—virtues and nonvirtues, as well as physical particles—may be complete, they lack a mind or consciousness. Without a conscious entity to empower them, they are unable to create their individual effects on their own. To empower them requires someone who is self-powered." They assert that such a person has the name "Īśvara, the divine creator of the world," and so on. Regarding this, the *Compendium of Reality* states:

> Others say that the cause
> of all products is Īśvara.
> An entity that has no consciousness
> cannot create its own effect.[26]

Furthermore, they point out, "Pots, houses, and so on have a variety of specific shapes that are formed from the different shapes of their components. Just from seeing these, we are able to automatically understand that a conscious entity created them. Likewise, because the locales, bodies, and so on of the world come in a variety of different shapes, this proves that their creation issued from the will of a divine creator." The *Compendium of Reality* states:

Those things that feature
shapes created from the shapes of their components
are produced by a cause that has consciousness.
This is like pitchers and so forth.[27]

And:

Just by seeing, you can tell there is a conscious entity.[28]

Moreover, they say, "Virtuous causes, nonvirtuous causes, and physical particles will sometimes remain without having created their effects— bodies and so forth. At some point, they will engage in the production of an effect. This is activated by a conscious entity—a divine creator." The *Compendium of Reality* states their position:

All virtuous causes, nonvirtuous causes, and particles
are empowered by a conscious entity,
or, like a loom, warp, and shuttle,
unless engaged in production, they simply remain idle.[29]

Another tradition asserts that there is no divine creator. The world arises, they say, from virtuous causes, nonvirtuous causes, and the "self" that assembles them. The followers of Īśvara say that this is not possible. They say that until a body, sense faculties, and so forth come together as cause and effect for that "self," there is no consciousness. On its own, the "self" does not have the power to take a fortunate or unfortunate rebirth. For this to happen it definitely must depend on the will of Īśvara. As cited in Kamalaśīla's *Compendium of Reality Commentary*, Bodhibhadra's *Explanation of Jñānagarbha's Compendium of the Essence of Wisdom* states this position as:

These persons have no consciousness.
They have no power to achieve their own happiness and suffering.
They can only go to high states or the abyss
if Īśvara sends them there.[30]

In short, the diverse phenomena that do not possess a mind—the elements of earth, water, fire, wind, and so on—do not become causes of happiness and suffering on their own. Only once a mental entity acts as a cause and empowers them do they become causes of happiness and suffering. Thus, they explain, you can clearly understand the existence of a divine creator of the world who is self-powered. The *Compendium of Reality* states:

> When a conscious entity empowers
> diverse phenomena such as the great elements,
> they become causes of the happiness
> and suffering of the entire world.

> As that which does not have a mind cannot cause an effect
> and cannot cause destruction and so forth,
> you can clearly understand the existence of a divine creator,
> just as tools like hatchets need a conscious entity to work.[31]

Analyzing the Reasons for the Existence of a Divine Creator

Some of these above-mentioned proponents of a divine creator of the world say that the bodies and places of the world are preceded by the will of a creator because they have a variety of shapes and also because they sometimes lie inert and sometimes are activated. They give the activity of a hatchet and the creation of a clay pot as illustrations.

We can examine this position as follows. In general, if we are proving merely some preceding mental activity, then even Buddhists, who do not assert a divine creator of the world, assert this. Buddhists say that these various entities of the world and the beings who use them are created from causes that include beings, who are living and are the accumulators of karma, as well as their individual and collective virtuous and nonvirtuous karma. Therefore it is senseless to debate by establishing something that has already been established. The *Compendium of Reality* states:

> If, in general, you assert
> a living entity that precedes,
> we have no argument with that.
> The variety of entities is produced from karma.[32]

Further, even if you are proving that the world and its inhabitants are created by a preceding mind that is permanent, one cannot deduce the predicate of the probandum from your examples of a pitcher and so on, because they do not establish creation by a *permanent* mind of the being who is their creator. The *Compendium of Reality* states:

> If you are proving that a permanent mind precedes it,
> the example for the predicate does not include a permanent mind.[33]

Also, you are giving the proof that "the places, bodies, and resources of the world are preceded by the will of a divine creator, because they lie inert for a time and then are activated." With regard to the phrase, "preceded by the will of a divine creator," one might prove that this will itself is created by the will of another living creator. Then, although the divine creator of the world is, in stages, staying at rest for a time and then engaging in effects, his will is empowered by the preceding will of another divine creator. If this were not so, then there is no certainty as to the pervasion of your above-mentioned reason, or there is simply no pervasion.[34] If you assert that the divine creator is preceded by the will of another divine creator, there would necessarily be no end to these creators. The *Compendium of Reality* states:

> It is not established that things are created in dependence on
>   the permanent mind
> of a divine creator who is permanent, a partless whole, and who
>   knows how to create all,
> because this creator is not different[35]
> and the predicate has no proper example.[36]

Also, Dharmakīrti's *Commentary on Valid Cognition* states (2.10)

> Remaining inert for a time and then engaging in action, a variety
>   of shapes,
> and performing a function
> are: an accepted assertion, an example that is not established,
> and a pervasion that is in doubt.

We can also analyze the reason "because they have shape" as follows. If you propose shape in general in the reason, how is it true that when something has shape, it necessarily issues from the will of a divine creator? If you propose in the reason a shape that arises from the creative effort of a being, your reason is not sound nor does the reason express a quality of the subject (the locales, bodies, and so on) because all the places, bodies, and so on of the world do not have shapes that arise from the efforts of some person. Shapes such as mountains do not arise from the effort of a living being but arise from the elements.

Analysis of the Nature of a Divine Creator

If an authoritative being who knows how to create everything—a self-existent divine creator of the world—exists from beginingless time, such a being cannot have a nature that is either permanent or impermanent. Why not? Such a creator would have to cognize objects that undergo change—impermanent objects. As such, his valid cognitions of objects that are sometimes clear due to distance and so on and sometimes unclear would thereby be changing and unstable. Therefore, as this divine creator's mind is changing, he cannot be called permanent.

Such a self-existent creator who is an authoritative being cannot be impermanent either. Why? At no point in such a being's history of passing through cyclic existence would he or she have been benefited or harmed or would he or she have become virtuous by cultivating virtue or nonvirtuous by being caught in the afflictions. Nor would he or she be omniscient and free of attachment due to the production of a sequence of similar types[37] from beginningless time. Therefore there can be no authoritative being who is both a self-existent creator of the world and also impermanent in the sense of arising from a sequence of previous similar types.

Dharmakīrti's *Commentary on Valid Cognition* states (2.8):

> A permanent authoritative being cannot exist
> because he or she has valid cognitions that realize impermanent
>   objects.
> His perceiving consciousness is not stable
> because its objects are impermanent.

And also (2.9):

> Because he or she is not benefited by a variety of things,
> he or she is not an authoritative being who is impermanent.

Doubting the Existence of a Divine Creator

Living beings use the physical world, which then becomes their instrument, and from this interaction their happiness and suffering arises. If all of these things were created by a divine creator of the world, this creator would create such things out of compassion for beings, not for any personal gain. And if so, he or she would create what beings would want—birth into a higher life as a human or god and happiness within that birth. Why would he or she create what no one wants—the miserable realms and their suffering? Likewise, he or she would want to destroy the worlds and suffering that beings do not want. Why would he or she cause the destruction of that which beings do want—higher birth and its happiness? Moreover, those with compassion only want to free beings from suffering, from what they do not want; then it does not make sense that beings are looking for the cause of their suffering. Would it not contradict having impartial compassion toward all if this loving god were assailing certain beings with intense sufferings?

Rejoinder: Living beings perform virtuous and nonvirtuous actions. Based on this, the divine creator of the world causes them to be happy or undergo suffering.

Response: If that is the case, it is contradictory to say the divine creator of the world creates things independently, without depending on others. Furthermore, as there are no living beings prior to the divine creator of the world creating them, out of compassion for whom does the divine creator create the beings and their environment? Likewise, why would the divine creator of the world create nonvirtue from the outset? The *Compendium of Reality* states:

> If he or she created them out of compassion,
> beings would only be happy.
> Yet they are beset by untold sufferings,
> such as sickness, poverty, and sorrow.

After creating such a life,
how can we say that he or she is compassionate?
Before creation, there are no objects of compassion
    [i.e., living beings];
to be compassionate after creation makes no sense.[38]

And also:

If such a creator has compassion,
that compassion must be impartial.[39]

Moreover, if a divine creator of the world made this variety of environments and the beings within them, as well as their happiness and suffering in the experimental manner of a child at play, he or she would have to do so in reliance on a variety of methods that would sometimes involve production, sometimes abiding, and sometimes perishing. Therefore how could the creator be all-powerful, making everything without depending on anything else?[40]

Also, if the divine creator could create whatever trials or games in accordance with his wish, independently, then he or she would have to make them all at once.[41] But it also makes no sense if, in order to create something, the divine creator at one time does not have the power to do so and then later gains the power to do so, creating in stages, for, as the creator is permanent, he or she would not have even the slightest fluctuation in capacity to create that thing all the time, constantly, even in the past and in the future. The *Compendium of Reality* states:

If the divine creator engages in creation in the manner
    of a game,
then there can be no all-powerful master of play
because he or she would have to rely on
diverse strategies of play, like children.

If the creator has the power to make things
by being a player who likes to win
and doing what achieves that,
then he or she would have to create all of this at once.[42]

Furthermore, such a divine creator of the world is permanent in the sense of being unchanging from moment to moment. Therefore he would not use either things that are coemergent or had preceded him to create even the slightest new attribute other than what is presently there. How could the divine creator be dependent on something else? In short, if a permanent thing that is not created from causes and conditions itself were to create the causes that give rise to something else, it is pointless to ask whether that creation is done in stages or all at once. The *Compendium of Reality* states:

> Because Īśvara was not produced,
> he cannot be the cause of production,
> like a lotus in the sky.
> If he were otherwise, everything would be produced at once.
> Whatever is produced in stages
> does not have Īśvara as its cause.[43]

Rejoinder: The divine creator of the world can always produce all effects without experiencing the fluctuation of increase and decrease. The fault of producing all effects at one time does not occur. How does the creator produce effects? He does it by the power of his own wish.

Response: This raises the following problem. Things that are effects give or cease to give their effects depending on the persistence or cessation of the complete causes and conditions that produce them. How can they give or cease their effect in dependence on a wish alone? It is like this. The seeds of the fruit and so on produce a sprout—even without the wish of a creator— once the complete causes are assembled, whereon the capacity to produce the sprout (the effect) is unhindered.[44] If this capacity is hindered, the effect will not arise, no matter how hard someone might wish it. Regarding this the *Rice Seedling Sutra* states:

> Regarding that, it does not occur to the earth element, "I perform the function of supporting the seed." Similarly, it does not occur to the water element, "I moisten the seed." It does not occur to the fire element, "I mature the seed." It does not occur to the air element, "I open the seed." It does not occur to the space element, "I perform the function of not obstructing the seed." It does not occur to the season, "I perform the function of

transforming the seed." It does not occur to the seed, "I produce the sprout." It does not occur to the sprout, "I was produced by these conditions." However, when these conditions exist and the seed ceases, a sprout will be produced. Similarly, up to: When the flower exists, a fruit also will be produced.

Rejoinder: The divine creator does not produce the various things of this world out of compassion for beings or in the manner of a game. Rather, just as the great elements—earth and so on—engage in producing their respective effects, so also the divine creator of the world generates this variety of animate and inanimate things.

Response: That raises the following problem. If it were like that, then the arising of this variety of inanimate and animate objects would be only due to the activity of this divine creator. Moreover, such a creator would be able to create newly, without any previous existence, all animate or inanimate things at all times and in all places. If this were so, this single divine creator would have the total ability to instantly generate all that exists, any variety of animate or inanimate things, and this divine creator, having a permanent nature that is always unchanging, must therefore have such an ability constantly. If this were so, then as only this divine creator of the world exists, he or she must constantly be creating all effects without any interruption, for he or she has the complete capacity to produce these effects instantly, merely by existing.[45] Dharmakīrti's *Commentary on Valid Cognition* states (2.225):

> For something that has all the causes,
> how could the effects ever cease?

Rejoinder: Just as a spider creates its web and so on naturally, without having to produce its effects all at once, so the divine creator creates his effects naturally and does not need to produce effects instantly.

Response: This also is not tenable. A spider spins the threads of its web out of its desire to eat insects; it does not do so simply by nature. The *Compendium of Reality* states:

> A spider does not naturally desire
> to use its threads for a web.

Out of its desire to eat insects,
it creates a net from its saliva.[46]

Rejoinder: The divine creator does not produce the various things of this world out of compassion for beings or as a game. Instead, just as when those who wander somewhere without much forethought, proceeding without investigation and just doing it in any old way, so the divine creator of the world creates the world.

Response: Why then should thoughtful people keep in mind the words of this creator over and above the words of a common fool? The *Compendium of Reality* states:

If the creator's manner of engagement is thoughtless,
what can we say about his creation?
Even a fisherman[47] will not work
without first thinking it over.[48]

The Thought and Deeds of Those Who Do Not Assert a Divine Creator

Question: Although there is no self-existent, permanent divine creator of the world from the point of view of the Buddhists, the things of this world are not self-existent without any causes and conditions. What are their causes?

Answer: Living beings' consciousnesses create both positive and negative mental karma. Arising from that are the many physical and verbal karmic actions, both virtuous and nonvirtuous. From these come the locales, bodies, and so on that are the bases for beings' experience of happiness and suffering. When the beings use those bases, they experience happiness and suffering. Candrakīrti's *Entering the Middle Way* states (6.89):

Mind itself creates the great variety
of animate and inanimate worlds.
Buddha stated that all beings arise from karma.
There is no karma without the mind.

And also (6.86):

> From understanding the refutation of a permanent self
>   and a creator,
> one knows that the creator is merely the mind.

Mind is the creator of the world. Once this is seen, it becomes clear that a divine creator cannot take living beings and create for them their fortunate and unfortunate rebirths under his own power, like a potter takes a lump of clay and creates a pot.

At present the variety of conditions—fortunate and unfortunate rebirths, happiness and suffering, virtuous and nonvirtuous thoughts and deeds—arise from differences in the degree to which one was previously accustomed to virtuous and nonvirtuous physical, verbal, and mental acts. These will arise in the same way in the future too. Therefore, with great effort, we must examine ourselves every moment and become skilled at rooting out physical, verbal, and mental defilements. Then we must aim to free ourselves from the sufferings of unfortunate rebirths and birth, aging, sickness, and death. It is said that we must become our own protector and refuge. The *Dhammapada* states (12.4):

> You are your own protector;
> who else can become your protector?
> The skillful become their own protectors
> and attain their aims.

And also (25.21):

> You are your own protector;
> you are your own refuge.

Those who take up the creation of their own happiness and suffering must clear away their physical, verbal, and mental faults and make exceptional efforts to cultivate good deeds. Once this happens, those who wish to cast aside what they don't want and obtain what they do want will feel empowered and confident in their ability to accomplish things. For these people, the refutation of a divine creator and the establishment of the mind as the creator becomes ripe with meaning. Those who uphold as their refuge such physical, verbal, and mental practices will see inner and outer dependently arisen phenomena clearly and will successfully subdue their attachment to the world, their unhappiness, and so forth. They will then energetically sustain their mindfulness and introspection. Those who abide in this way will take as their refuge and haven principally themselves as well as their physical, verbal, and mental virtues. The Buddha said that these persons are the best students of what the Teacher has to teach. As the *Finer Points of Discipline* states:

> Ānanda, consequently, whether I am here or not, those who take their selves as their haven, their selves as their refuge, the practices as their haven, the practices as their refuge, finding no other haven and no other refuge, they are the best of my monks in training.[49]

Let's compare those who assert a divine creator to those who follow a teaching that does not assert such a creator. When we look at their beliefs, we find quite a difference in how they conceive and express their teachings. Yet, among those with a spiritual faith in general, whether they assert or do not assert a divine creator, we find fewer clear differences when we examine their thoughts and deeds. Among those with a good understanding of the view and tenets wherein a divine creator does not exist, many have thoughts and deeds that are indistinguishable from those who do assert a divine creator. For among those who do not assert a divine creator, many do assert virtuous and nonvirtuous karma to be the creator of happiness and suffering, and these people consequently strive to eliminate sin and cultivate virtue. Thus, even if a creator were to exist, these people would be acting in accord with his intention.

Not everyone who does not believe in a divine creator is a nihilist like the Cārvākas. Buddhists do not assert a divine creator, but they do assert a Teacher (Buddha) who is a refuge, one with the power of having completely eliminated faults and realized all good qualities, fulfilling others' aims. Tibetan and other Buddhists also assert a spectrum of deities who can intercede in matters of wealth, lifespan, peace, growth, power, fierceness, and so forth. Therefore one aspect of their way of thinking accords with those who believe in a divine creator.

Nevertheless, among those powerful deities, none is a divine creator of the world. Also buddhas such as the Blessed One are teachers who show the way to genuine refuge and are the ultimate refuge, but the Buddha is not a divine creator of the world. Buddhists refute the assertions of other traditions that a great deity such as Brahmā or Īśvara is the divine creator of the world. So although there are Buddhists who assert the existence of great deities, they do not accept that these deities are creators.

Question: Buddhist scriptures disagree with proponents of a divine creator and spend much time analyzing the issue. Are Buddhists hostile toward others' philosophical stances?

Answer: The point of these analyses is to understand for oneself whether a divine creator exists. It is not to generate hostility toward others. The Teacher, Buddha, stated that his disciples should thoroughly examine his teachings well and accept them once they have eliminated any doubt. The Buddha did not want his disciples to engage with his words out of faith and admiration alone, accepting them merely because the Buddha spoke them. Wanting to enhance his disciples' intelligence, the Buddha told them to accept his teachings only after examining his words closely. The *Tantra of Very Powerful Glory* states:

> Analyze my words well as one would analyze gold
> through melting, refining, and polishing, and adopt them then.
> The skilled should not engage them
> out of admiration or for other reasons.[50]

Furthermore, when you analyze scriptures in order to understand their meaning, you shouldn't identify a person with that analysis and become attached to or hostile toward that person. Even if someone harms you in anger, the Buddha said that, rather than viewing the person as your enemy and returning the anger, you should view the anger as your enemy and strive to destroy it. In this vein Āryadeva's *Four Hundred Stanzas* says (5.109):

> Just as a physician is not upset with
> someone who rages while possessed by a demon,
> sages see the afflictions as the enemy,
> not the person who has them.

And just as it is incorrect to get angry at and hate those who harm you in that way, it is said that it is also incorrect to nurse resentment for those who criticize the Buddha's teaching and images of the Three Jewels—statues of the Buddha, the stupa at Bodhgaya, and so forth—as well as those who physically destroy those objects. Why? The people who do these things cannot harm the buddhas and so forth with their destructive actions. Under the power of their ignorance, attachment, and hostility, they are unable to maintain their usual state of mind, and it is as if they have become crazy. Seeing this, they should become for you objects of compassion. Śāntideva's *Engaging in the Bodhisattva's Deeds* states (6.64):

> Should others talk badly or even destroy
> holy images, reliquaries, and the sacred teaching,
> it is improper for me to resent it,
> for the buddhas can never be injured.[51]

While some religions assert a divine creator, others like the Buddhists assert that karma is the creator of the world. However, those with faith in the teachings of the former, striving to act in accord with the intention of their creator, cast aside sin and cultivate virtue. Those with faith in the law of karma also make effort to cast aside sin and cultivate virtue, recognizing the role of virtuous and nonvirtuous thoughts and deeds in creating their happiness and suffering. So whether you assert a divine creator of the world or you assert karma as the cause of the world, you are the same in striving at this important foundation of casting aside wrongdoing and practicing good deeds.

Question: The various religions that assert a divine creator of the world share a similar way of thinking. Are they all branches of one religion?

Answer: It seems that they must be if you look at how they are actually related. For example, individuals give different names to the same object, like when "blaze" and "fire" are both understood to refer to only one object. Likewise, the various theistic religions use different names for the divine creator of the world, yet the referent of their names must all be the same thing.

Nevertheless, those who have faith in the existence of a creator god tend to think that, while the individual religions have different names for the divine creator, the divine creator is exclusive to their particular religion; they do not think that he or she is shared with all religions. Accordingly, they believe that the divine creator that they call by the name associated with their particular religion is the protector of the people of their own religion and is not the protector of those who have faith in some other religion. They also think, for instance, that the world protector who is called a certain name by other religions protects and gratifies those others but not themselves.

If there were actually world protectors for each religion that asserts them, there would necessarily be a variety of world protectors. Also, the happiness and pleasure of those who assert no divine creator would either have to be created by a generic divine creator or not be created by any creator at all.

Therefore, for anyone who asserts a divine creator of the world, it is not possible to have one creator for oneself and many for others. The very creator that one asserts must be the creator of all beings and their environment. All the religions and those who have faith in their teachings must be created by the will of the one creator. Thus the one creator god created with his will all the different religions, all the followers of those various faiths, or and even those with no faith and no religion. As this creator takes responsibility for that, anyone with faith in the teachings of any religion must accept the will of the divine creator of the world and hold no one to be an enemy and instead take responsibility for them.

Further, it was long ago in India, the land of the noble beings, that there appeared a religion that asserted a self-existent divine creator of the world who was called by names such as Iśvāra. In harmony with the dispositions of many people, this tradition has been greatly helpful, promoting happiness and well-being. In addition, six centuries before the common era, the Buddha, the Blessed One, visited this world and revealed a different explanation for the world's existence: the great variety of worlds arose primarily from living beings' virtuous and nonvirtuous actions of body, speech, and mind. What was his purpose in teaching this?

The people of this world think in diverse ways owing to their different dispositions and beliefs. Had happiness and suffering, as well as the resources that are the bases for those, been allocated by a divine creator from time immemorial, and if this situation had to remain like that, some people might despair. They might think that they are themselves powerless to eliminate all their faults and achieve all good qualities. However, were they able to see that they have the capacity to be their own refuge, their courage would increase, and they would make an exceedingly great effort to cultivate virtue. Understanding this, the Buddha clarified this truth of karma.

If a person who has perfect knowledge and compassion and strives for others' happiness and benefit does exist, this person must first have passed through cyclic existence like ourselves and have once possessed ignorance, attachment, and hostility. Then this person would have to have exclusively made great effort over a long time to abandon those faults to now be a person who has perfect good qualities of knowledge and abandonment. In the same way, we who pass through cyclic existence also have the potential to become a buddha, the ability to perfect the good qualities of knowledge and abandonment. The nature of our mind is clear light, and our defilements are adventitious. Therefore we can transform ourselves like that. Just as the pure nature of the sky and water can, respectively, become free of dust and mud, our minds can become free of defilements.

Consequently, we do not need someone else to determine whether we will be good or evil in the future; we can do it ourselves now. We are our own refuge and protector. Seeing this, we must make a great effort to eliminate the cause of those faults—the ignorance of not knowing—and through love and compassion abandon harming others and provide them help and happiness. Those who do so are in complete accord with the intention of every perfect being there is who is consistently helping living beings. Therefore it is an offering that brings these ultimate sources of refuge only superior reverence and pleasure. It is not like this for those who harm living beings. It is just as Nāgārjuna says in *Verses on Respecting Living Beings*:

> To be of the utmost help to living beings is the best way to venerate me.
> To greatly harm living beings is the greatest harm to me.
> Living beings and I are the same in wanting happiness and not wanting suffering;
> how can whoever harms living beings be respecting me?[52]

So long as the precious teaching of the Buddha is evident in this world, we should offer the utmost help—maintaining an impartial attitude without being partisan, thinking "us" and "them." The Buddha brings joy—

freedom from sorrow—to living beings for their welfare. He says that there is no point for those who bring living beings sorrow and suffering to even sustain their own bodies with food. In this vein, *Verses on Respecting Living Beings* states:

> So long as my teaching is clearly present in this world,
> offer the greatest help: impartiality toward all.
> For those who bring sorrow to living beings, to whom I equally
> bring joy for their welfare, there is no point in even sustaining
>   their bodies with food![53]

Furthermore, a saying of the Kadam geshes states that two sources of merit are crucial for those who wish to attain liberation and omniscience. First is the Buddha, who shows the path. Second, in accord with the path shown by the Teacher, is living beings, who are both to be freed from suffering and to be imbued with happiness. For living beings are the objects of compassion, which is the wish to free others from suffering, and the objects of love, which is the wish to provide them with happiness.

It then states that for those who want liberation and omniscience, the primary source to cherish between these two is living beings. Why? In this life and in all former lives, living beings have sustained us with kindness, having been our parents, relatives, and the like. Although living beings were not powerlessly made to suffer by someone else—they created their own suffering—they are nonetheless helpless. As we must help them, we must cherish them.

Moreover, not only do we achieve our own aim of liberation and omniscience by helping living beings, we also make the supreme offering that pleases and gladdens all the buddhas and bodhisattvas of the ten directions, who hold living beings to be more precious than themselves. Therefore we must cherish living beings more than buddhas. Those who do this reach the very heart of the Buddha's intention and thus exceptionally please him. How could it displease him? As it says in *Sayings of the Kadam Masters*:

> Again, the spiritual mentor Chengawa said: "To attain liberation and omniscience, you must train in a practice that is at variance with what worldly people do. For instance, the worldly cherish the buddhas more than living beings, they cherish them-

selves more than others, they cherish those who help them more than those who cause them harm, and they cherish pleasure more than hardship.

"Given that we must act in an inverse manner, we must cherish living beings more than the buddhas. Why? Because normally not even the slightest disrespect will arise toward the buddhas."[54]

Also, Śāntideva's *Engaging in the Bodhisattva's Deeds* states (6.113):

A buddha's qualities are attained
from living beings and conquerors alike,
so why do I not respect living beings
in the same way as I respect the conquerors?

3. Is Dependently Arisen Production Actual Production?

———— •◆• ————

Different Positions on Dependent Arising

In the *Sutra Proclaiming the Lion's Roar*, in the context of explaining external and internal dependent arisings, the Buddha says that they are "neither self-generated nor other-generated."[55] In addition, he states, "Whether tathāgatas appear or not, the nature of phenomena remains."[56] Citing these passages from scripture, the Mahīśāsakas, one of the early Buddhist sects, held the position that dependent arising is uncompounded and permanent. This is according to the master Vasubandhu's *Treasury of Knowledge Autocommentary*[57] and Yaśomitra's *Extensive Commentary on the Treasury of Knowledge*.[58]

All the schools of Buddhist essentialists other than the Mahīśāsakas, however, assert that all dependently arisen phenomena are compounded phenomena produced from their respective causes. They say that the two scriptural references, though seeming to suggest that dependent arising is permanent and uncompounded, actually mean that the cyclic existence into which living beings of the six types are born and within which they live does not arise causelessly and is not the creation of a discordant cause—a permanent, self-existent creator. Cyclic existence, they say, arises by way of the sequential production of twelve factors of dependent arising, beginning with ignorance. The sutra says that this process is a natural law, one that functions whether or not tathāgathas appear. Vasubandhu's *Treasury of Knowledge Autocommentary* states, "If you were to say that the intention [of the sutra] is that whether or not tathāgathas appear in the world, the factors of dependent arising, such as conditioning factors (*saṃskārakarma*), always arise in dependence on other factors, such as ignorance (*avidyā*), and do not arise without dependence or without depending on something else and that dependent arising is permanent in this sense, then I, too, would stand by your assertion." The text further states, "If you were to say that a functional thing could have even the slightest aspect of permanence, I would have to reject your position and say that it is not so."[59] The *Autocommentary* also confirms that, except for the Mahīśāsakas, all Buddhist essentialists assert that anything dependently arisen is necessarily compounded.

Many Tibetan scholars, including the master Tsongkhapa, accept that when, in the opening homage of the *Fundamental Verses on the Middle Way*, Nāgārjuna says, "Whatever is dependently arisen," this means that any dependent arising used as the basis for repudiating functions such as arising, ceasing, and so forth must be a compounded dependent arising. They also maintain, however, that the Madhyamaka system's presentation of dependent arising differs from that of the essentialists in that dependent arising is not confined to compounded phenomena, which are produced from their respective causes and conditions, but also includes uncompounded phenomena such as space. Such Mādhyamikas assert that, even though space does not arise from its respective causes, it is established in dependence on its basis of imputation and, as such, is an uncompounded dependent arising. Therefore, in the Madhyamaka system, every phenomenon is a dependent arising.

They also say that the word *dependent* in *dependent arising* means both "contingent" and "linked." Therefore the meaning of the word *dependent* is present in all phenomena. The word *arising* conveys two meanings: production and establishment. Thus, even when a phenomenon is not produced in dependence on some other thing, it nevertheless is established, or arises, in dependence on that thing. The *Fundamental Verses on the Middle Way* (8.12) says:

> Agent depends on action.
> Action depends on the agent as well.
> Apart from dependent arising,
> one cannot see any way they are established.

According to the Madhyamaka system, although agent and action have not necessarily produced each other, they do arise in mutual dependence. The master Nāgārjuna's *Precious Garland* states (1.48):

This arises because of the existence of that;
for example, short exists because of long.

Nāgārjuna is saying that long does not produce short, but short never-theless arises from long. His *Fundamental Verses on the Middle Way* (8.13cd) says:

Through the example of action and agent,
all remaining things should be understood.

In the commentary on the above lines, the master Candrakīrti's *Clear Words* says, "In addition to the agent and the action, and the appropriated and the appropriator, the wise should refute, through analyzing action and agent, the essential existence of all composite phenomena, such as the produced and the producer, the going and the goer, the seen and the one who sees, the definition and the definiendum, the arising and the agent of arising, the components and the whole, the quality and the possessor of qualities, the valid cognizer and the object validly cognized, and so forth, understanding that they are established only through mutual dependency."[60] Thus Candra-kīrti gives many examples of dependent arisings, both compounded and uncompounded phenomena, whose identities are established in mutual dependence on each other.

Furthermore, the Buddha said that all phenomena are dependent aris-ings established in dependence on their respective bases of imputation and imputed terms and concepts. As it says in sutra:

Just as one speaks of a chariot
in dependence upon collections of parts,
so we use the convention "living being"
in dependence upon the aggregates.[61]

We establish the existence of a chariot through labeling by terms and con-cepts, saying "This is a chariot" in dependence on the parts of a chariot—the wheels and so forth. The Buddha points out that we likewise establish the existence of a person by merely labeling "This is a person" in dependence on its basis of imputation, the aggregates.

Therefore all phenomena are dependent arisings established in dependence on their parts and the imputation of conventions. Moreover, when we search for the object of the label "This is a pitcher" and ask, "What is the pitcher?" we do not find anything that is the pitcher within those parts—such as its bulbous base—that constitute its cause or its basis of imputation, nor do we find anything that is the pitcher anywhere separate from the parts. Thus the pitcher does not exist from its own side. Nonetheless, the manner in which the pitcher, which is able to perform the function of holding water and so forth, is completed is by merely affixing the label "This is a pitcher" with a mind that imputes based on the pitcher's basis of imputation.

This way of positing dependent arising as mere dependent imputation is unique to the system of the Prāsaṅgika Mādhyamikas. The master Candrakīrti's *Commentary on the Four Hundred Stanzas* states:

> A pitcher and so forth are not found to exist on application of the fivefold analysis to determine whether they are one with their "cause" [i.e., their basis of imputation] or other than their basis of imputation. Nonetheless, as dependent imputations, they are capable of such functions as holding and dispensing honey, water, milk, and so forth. How amazing is this![62]

In this manner, dependently arisen phenomena are free of the extreme of permanence because they are devoid of independent existence or existence from their own side. Though lacking any objective existence, they are not completely nonexistent because they are capable of functioning. One can posit that they exist as mere designations, imputed by terms and concepts in dependence on their bases of imputation. This is said to be the "middle path" free of the two extremes of permanence and annihilation. Therefore, since all phenomena are dependent arisings, they lack existence from their own side.

The *Fundamental Verses on the Middle Way* (24.18–19) states:

> Whatever is dependently arisen,
> that is explained to be emptiness.
> That, being a dependent imputation,
> is itself the middle way.

Something that is not dependently arisen,
such a thing does not exist.
Therefore a nonempty thing
does not exist.

It is likewise stated in the *Perfection of Wisdom Sutra in 100,000 Verses,* "Everything exists by the power of the world's conventions, not by ultimate existence."[63] Candrakīrti's *Commentary on the Four Hundred Stanzas* states: "Therefore, everything exists only by conceptuality and cannot exist without it. Without a doubt, everything lacks essential existence, just as a snake imputed on a coiled rope."[64] Thus no phenomenon exists independently. All phenomena are established as arising in dependence on their parts, on their bases of imputation, and on imputed terms and concepts.

PROPONENTS OF DEPENDENT ARISING

Whereas proponents of Buddhist tenets assert that all composite things, both animate and inanimate, arise in dependence on merely their respective causes and conditions, proponents of non-Buddhist tenets do not assert such a dependent arising. Their assertions are as follows. Cārvākas hold that the world and its inhabitants were self-existent from the beginning, produced without any cause. Sāṅkhyas assert that an effect, which is of the same nature as its cause, exists concurrently with this permanent cause but in a nonmanifest manner. This effect is later produced again such that it becomes manifest. Still others hold that things are produced from the outset by a single, permanent cause, whether this cause be (1) a permanent entity called "time," which is an intrinsically established cause with a different nature from its effect; (2) a permanent, partless, atom-like particle serving as the building block of the entire world system; or (3) a self-existent, permanent divine creator. These proponents of non-Buddhist tenets assert that once the things that are the effects have been produced, their entities remain without perishing each moment. When such effects finally do perish, they either dissolve back into their initial cause or are withdrawn by their divine creator.

From the Madhyamaka perspective, if an effect were to be produced in the manner that such non-Buddhists assert, it would be produced either causelessly or from discordant causes. Because such a position runs counter to the view that effects arise in dependence on concordant causes and conditions, such non-Buddhists are not proponents of dependent arising.

By contrast, all proponents of Buddhist tenets propound dependent arising. They do not accept that the world and its inhabitants came into being in the ways asserted by non-Buddhists described above. Rather, they hold that, with no permanent, unchanging entity as their cause, phenomena arise from an aggregation of numerous causes and conditions. That is, an effect arises from both its substantial cause that generates its respective form and cooperative conditions that simultaneously assist the substantial cause in becoming the entity that is its effect. Furthermore, once an effect is produced and abides, it cannot remain without undergoing change. Immediately upon being produced, an effect has an impermanent nature that changes moment to moment. When it disintegrates, it perishes either due to the absence of causes and conditions capable of generating the subsequent moment of similar type in its continuum or due to meeting with some other unfavorable condition that interrupts its continuity.

In summary, a composite thing that is an effect does not arise from a permanent cause or from a divine creator's will. Rather, it arises and perishes in dependence on the presence or absence of the many impermanent causes and conditions that have a concordant capacity to produce it. Whether in the beginning, middle, or end, it is never possible for the effect to exist both as a composite entity and as a permanent and unchanging one.

Qualm: From the viewpoint of the Prāsaṅgika Madhyamaka system, the two Buddhist schools asserting external existence (the Vaibhāṣika and Sautrāntika schools) and the Cittamātra school would not be proponents of dependent arising, for both the Vaibhāṣika and the Sautrāntika assert an external reality produced from virtuous and nonvirtuous causes that are truly established and capable of bearing analysis, and the Cittamātra assert a truly established foundation consciousness (*ālayavijñāna*) capable of withstanding analysis and serving as the basis for retaining karmic predispositions. According to Prāsaṅgika Mādhyamikas, composite things are not inherently, or truly, established, and therefore such a presentation of the dependent arising of cause and effect would be untenable. The *Fundamental Verses on the Middle Way* (15.1–2) states:

> It makes no sense to say that intrinsic nature
> is produced from causes and conditions.

If produced from causes and conditions,
intrinsic nature would be a product.

How could it be appropriate
for intrinsic nature to be a product?
For intrinsic nature is not created;
nor does it depend on another.

Reply: In general, as explained above, these Buddhist essentialists them-selves claim to uphold the principle of dependent arising and accept that the world and its inhabitants arise from the three, or five, conditions, such as the lack of a divine creator's will. Regarding their assertions, however, Tsongkhapa states in his *Praise of Dependent Arising* (verse 6):

The immature who hold on to this
strengthen the bonds of extremism;
for the wise this very thing is the way
to cut the net of elaborations.

For the essentialists, the dependently arisen nature of composite things entails that they are truly established in order to be able to perform func-tions. Thus they uphold dependent arising as the reason composite things are truly established. According to Tsongkhapa, in so arguing they strengthen the bonds of the extreme of permanence. In contrast, the wise Mādhyamikas argue that, because of being dependently arisen, composite things must *not* be truly existent and must *not* exist from their own side. They contend that, although composite things do not truly or inherently exist, they nevertheless are able to perform all functions. Therefore Tsongkhapa states that, for the Mādhyamikas, dependent arising becomes the way to cut the entire net of conceptuality rooted in the apprehension of true existence.

Thus, while Buddhist essentialists rely on the Buddhist path that pro-pounds dependent arising, they in turn critique the Mādhyamikas, who assert that composite things lack a truly established essence, and they stand firm in their proud assertion that composite things are truly established and exist by way of their own essence. For this reason, according to the Mādhyamikas, Buddhist essentialists do not precisely understand or competently propound subtle dependent arising. Tsongkhapa says in his *Essence of Eloquence*:

> It is not at all surprising that non-Buddhists, who assert that composite things are permanent, do not accept dependent arising and therefore assert that phenomena are truly established. This is their teacher's position. However, it is absurd to accept, on the one hand, dependent arising, wherein things arise and are produced in dependence on causes and conditions, and on the other hand, to uphold that phenomena are truly established.[65]

The master Nāgārjuna's *Sixty Stanzas of Reasoning* says:

> When the [non-Buddhist] proponents of [true] existence
> abide by clinging to truly existent things as superior,
> there is nothing to be surprised about,
> for they live by such a path.
>
> Those who rely on the Buddhist path
> and propound the impermanence of all things
> but, in debate, take the position of true existence
> and hold to it are deplorable.[66]

Similarly, the great Gorampa said that although non-Buddhists do not accept dependent arising and Buddhist essentialists are proponents of dependent arising, the latter do not comprehend dependent arising precisely.[67] Khedrup Je, however, says in his *Dose of Emptiness*: "Except for those who assert that composite things are produced causelessly, all other philosophical systems are already aware of the presence of the reason in the subject (*pakṣadharma*) in a syllogism that uses the reason of dependent arising. Thus there is no need to establish it for them."[68] Likewise, Panchen Shakya Chokden says:

> Even the worldly non-Buddhists
> speak of dependent arising,

for they say that effects arise from causes.
To deny this would be absurd.[69]

Thus it is said that except for those non-Buddhists who accept causeless production, non-Buddhists also understand and explain that effects arise from causes and therefore comprehend and propound dependent arising. This requires examination. The master Karmapa Mikyö Dorje says, "Buddhists and non-Buddhists who accept production from any of the four possibilities or any of the eight possibilities are not proponents of dependent arising. In addition, they are neither proponents of emptiness nor proponents of the Middle Way."[70]

My view is as follows. The *Rice Seedling Sutra* cited earlier[71] states that the definition of the dependent arising of composite phenomena is production from five or three conditions, such as multiple and impermanent conditions, conditions that have a capacity for production, and no production from a divine creator's will. Furthermore, another sutra states:

Just as one speaks of a chariot
in dependence upon collections of parts,
so we use the convention "living being"
in dependence upon the aggregates.[72]

Here the Buddha indicates that a dependent arising is established in dependence on its basis of imputation and the imputation of terms and concepts. Non-Buddhists do not know this meaning of dependent arising and are not proponents of it, for they assert that this world of true suffering is produced from a cause that is ultimately partless, permanent, and unitary, such as a permanent cause that has the same nature as its effect or a cause that is the will of a permanent divine creator. From this perspective, non-Buddhist teachers are not proponents of dependent arising. Thus it is entirely fitting to attribute the teaching of dependent arising to our teacher, the Buddha, Master of the Sages. This is stated in the master Nāgārjuna's *Hymn to the World Transcendent*:

Dialecticians assert that suffering is created by itself;
created by another, by both self and another,

or that they have no cause at all.
You have stated it to be dependent arising.

That which originates through dependence,
this you maintain to be empty;
that no independent entity exists,
you, the Peerless One, proclaimed in a lion's roar.[73]

Also, in his *Verses on the Rice Seedling Sutra*, the master Nāgārjuna says:

Nothing is produced from itself or from other,
from both, or from "time,"
from a divine creator, such as Īśvara,
from a principal nature, or without a cause.

An arising from causes and conditions
comes from beginningless time;
thus, you assert that external things arise
in dependence on the five causes.[74]

The Assertion That a Dependently Arisen Production Is Not an Actual Production

Qualm: The Prāsaṅgika Madhyamaka system explains arising and ceasing with respect to dependent arising. Is dependently arisen production, therefore, genuine production?

Reply: On this question, some scholars assert production that is not genuine and other scholars assert production that is genuine. I will say a little about the former position based mainly on the statements of the master Karmapa Mikyö Dorje but on others as well.

Assertions of the Master Karmapa Mikyö Dorje

According to Karmapa Mikyö Dorje, when the Buddha states in the *Rice Seedling Sutra* that dependent arising is "just these conditions," he points out that when such things as sprouts are produced, they arise from causes and conditions that are seen by and known to the world. He clearly indicates that a sprout does not arise from those causes postulated by Buddhist essentialist and non-Buddhist tenets.[75] Moreover, although in reality production is baseless, from the perspective of the world there is no other way than to posit causes and effects, arising and ceasing. Therefore scholars such as Karmapa Mikyö Dorje assert the perspective of others—that is, worldly persons.

Furthermore, it is not the case that an existent production, on analysis, becomes nonexistent, for there was no production in the first place. However, this does not contradict the appearance of a dependently arisen production. Although in actuality there is no production or cessation, there is an appearance of the dependent arising of production and cessation according to the perspective of worldly persons. This is mistaken production and cessation. Thus, positing a dependently arisen production and cessation is merely in compliance with what is commonly accepted by others.[76]

Although production is not established at all, the appearance of production and cessation in dependent arising is nevertheless possible. It is analogous to the unchanging, natural emptiness of the sky, in which, though there is nothing at all, it is still feasible for a great variety of things, such as a change in the light due to clouds, a dust storm, sunlight, or darkness, to appear. Likewise, a magician's horse, elephant, or other creation appears, even though there is no actual horse or other object existing at the site of the appearance. So it is feasible for anything—a horse or an elephant, for example—to appear.

No dependently arisen phenomena can be established or asserted in accordance with a Buddha's way of seeing things. All the varieties of production and so forth of conventional phenomena are feasible only as mere appearances to worldly persons.

Qualm: If production is without basis in the Madhyamaka system, just as production from the four alternatives is refuted, isn't production also refuted?

Answer: As there is no production other than production from the four alternatives, not only is the ultimate existence of production and production from the four alternatives refuted, but also their conventional existence is refuted.

Qualm: Would one then say that the Mādhyamikas do not even posit dependently arisen production and so forth?

Answer: In the Prāsaṅgika Madhyamaka system, if one were to establish production by reason of its being a dependent arising, one would incur the fault of giving a contradictory reason, which entails a wrong pervasion. They do not assert that dependently arisen production is actual production. If dependently arisen production were posited as genuine production, then the Prāsaṅgika Madhyamaka would incur the fault of first *refuting* the view of the essentialists that production and cessation are valid and genuine by reason of any of the four alternatives, and then *positing* that there is real production and real cessation by reason of dependent arising. This would be like an elephant's bath: he washes, rolls in the dirt, and then washes again. These two views—real production from one of the four alternatives and dependently arisen production—are similar in that they are both bonds. It is like the saying that, whether one is bound by a golden chain or an iron chain, one is still bound by a chain.[77]

Therefore dependent arising is said to refer to the negation of production from causes and conditions. Some scholars say that the meaning of dependent arising is production from causes and conditions. They are wrong. They make meaningless statements, such as: "When Mādhyamikas do analysis, they refute production that falls into one of the extremes, but they do not refute dependently arisen production." Or "Although Mādhyamikas refute production from the four alternatives, they assert dependently arisen production conventionally." Those who make such statements hold on to the production and cessation of things just as they seem to them and do not want to let go of what exists in their minds, obscuring the liberating view of the Mādhyamikas. By positing the possibility of dependently arisen production, cessation, and so forth in their system, they do not even have the scent of a Mādhyamika.[78]

Nevertheless, the Mādhyamikas who assert dependent arising do so without falling outside of the two truths. By saying that all mundane and supramundane conventions are feasible in the appearance of dependent arising, they do not fall outside of conventional truths. And because they do not hold on to anything by not falling into any of the four alternatives (self, other, and so on) or the eight alternatives (of production, cessation, and so forth), they do not fall outside of the ultimate truth either.

Qualm: Are those who assert dependent arising without falling outside of the two truths really Mādhyamikas?

Answer: They are Prāsaṅgika Mādhyamikas only for others who give arguments and merely label them "Prāsaṅgika Mādhyamikas." Prāsaṅgika

Mādhyamikas themselves do not assert that such proponents are Prāsaṅgika Mādhyamikas.

Qualm: Why do you refer to them as Mādhyamikas?

Answer: In order to have an opportunity to debate with you, I conform to your term because you want to use it. Once I have left the debate and am not under its pressure, I would never think or say, "I am a Mādhyamika." Even during the debate, I do not think of or use such an expression, even though it appears that I am doing so. This is just like an echo.[79]

Assertions of Other Scholars

According to Mipham Rinpoche, it is not the case that a pitcher, for instance, exists before it is analyzed with reasons and then becomes empty when subjected to analysis, as if it were destroyed with a hammer or burned in a fire, like wood. If this were so, then after you realized emptiness, there would be no pitcher to appear to one's mind, or it would not be capable of appearing to your mind. Rather, you must understand that a pitcher appears while being empty and is empty while appearing.[80]

With the above-mentioned views in mind, the great scholar Gendun Chophel says in his *Ornament to the Intent of Nāgārjuna* that when one applies rational analysis, one does not need to set aside illusion-like dependent arisings but must use the analysis to refute all appearances. However, it is certain that some illusion-like thing will remain after the analysis. To give an analogy, when one burns a mixture of things such as gold, clods of earth, dirt, stones, and twigs, those things that are flammable will burn, but those things that are inflammable will remain.[81]

The Jonang master Dolpopa Sherab Gyaltsen states that dependent arisings must be compounded, deceptive, and false phenomena that are self-empty—they don't exist; whereas the sphere of reality, emptiness, is nondeceptive and true. Therefore it is the ultimate truth and other-empty. It is neither self-empty nor a dependent arising.[82] In other words, for Dolpopa, there is only ultimate truth, and the only thing it is empty of is everything that is other than ultimate truth.

The great scholar Shakya Chokden maintains that to say that emptiness is a dependent arising is contradictory, because emptiness is free of all elaborations. He also says that mutual dependence is a proof that something does not exist. Therefore, he maintains that dependently arisen production and the like do not prove the existence of production and so forth. How is this so? Contingent existence and conventional existence are not capable of establishing the existence of anything. If dependently arisen conventionalities such as karma and its effects existed, then they would not be illusion-like, for the meaning of "illusion-like" is that something that does not exist nevertheless appears. If conventionalities existed, they would be the object of a buddha's omniscience, but ultimate existence is the object of a buddha's omniscience, and conventionalities never appear to it. Therefore, because a buddha does not see dependently arisen conventionalities, when some scholars explain the knowledge of dependent arising by means of omniscience as being a peerless knowledge, they are incorrect. Thus there is no distinction between existence and inherent existence, and it is also unsuitable to distinguish nonexistence from noninherent existence,[83] as do Tsongkhapa and his followers.

Dependently Arisen Production Is Actual Production

Production and so forth of dependently arisen composite things appears to the conventional consciousnesses of ordinary beings. Je Tsongkhapa and others assert that while such appearances are mistaken, composite things have actual production and each thing is able to perform functions. Drawing on Tsongkhapa's teachings in the insight section of the *Great Treatise on the Stages of the Path to Enlightenment*, I will further clarify the meaning of this assertion.

First, let's look at what is taught in the sutras. This appearance of production, cessation, and so forth to an ordinary person's consciousness is not an erroneous appearance of something that is completely nonexistent. However, whenever any conventional phenomenon—such as production—appears to a living being's consciousness, it appears to be established not as dependently arisen but from its own side. Although all composite things are established in dependence on their causes and conditions and their parts, they do not appear in this way to a direct perception. Rather, they appear to be established independently. Due to the independent way objects appear to such cognitions, these appearances are mistaken.

Furthermore, it is said in the *King of Concentration Sutra*:

How can one say that an object appears mistakenly when the mind has no basis for it being mistaken? It is as follows: Do not think that phenomena existing and appearing as mere illusion-like conventions is an appearance to an erroneous mind. Rather, understand that the mistaken appearance of phenomena as permanent and enduring, without knowing their lack of inherent production, is how the object appears to a mistaken mind.[84]

Again, the same sutra says:

Mañjuśrī! In short, by not knowing that phenomena lack inherent production and then apprehending them as permanent and enduring, one passes through cyclic existence. This is how phenomena appear to a mistaken mind. However, it is not the case that an erroneous mind causes phenomena to appear from an original state of nonexistence that is like space.[85]

The Tibetan words *takpa* (*rtag pa*) and *tersuk* (*ther zug*) sometimes have the same meaning and sometimes have a different meaning. When synonymous, *takpa* and *tersuk* both mean "unchanging." In the context of this sutra citation, the Buddha uses the phrase "apprehending phenomena as permanent (*takpa*) and enduring (*tersuk*)" in reference to phenomena appearing to be inherently established and then apprehending them to be so. The Buddha made this statement because once phenomena exist inherently, they must remain without changing. It is as if the Buddha first explained that the extreme of permanence refers to phenomena existing inherently and then said that the "view of permanence" refers to the view of this extreme. There are other instances where *takpa* and *tersuk* must be interpreted to have different meanings. *Takpa* refers to a former phenomenon abiding in the present without having changed. *Tersuk* refers to a present phenomenon remaining in the future without undergoing change.

In keeping with the sutra passage above, the glorious Candrakīrti states in his *Commentary on the Four Hundred Stanzas*:

Qualm: If there is no inherent existence, what does exist?
Answer: I will explain. Phenomena that serve as the sources

of virtues and afflictions exist; they are similar to illusion-like
elephants, horses, and so forth. Ordinary persons mistakenly
understand them to have inherent existence. Noble beings
(*āryas*) precisely understand them to lack inherent existence and
to be like a magician's illusions, a mirage, and so forth.[86]

Just as it is said in the above sutras and commentaries, whatever appears to
us—such as the production of phenomena and so forth—appears to exist
inherently and to exist from its own side, and we then apprehend it as such.[87]
If a phenomenon that appears to us to exist from its own side did indeed
exist in this way, then, just as the essentialists assert, by examining and searching for the object implied by the conventions "this is an aggregate" or "this is
a person," we would be able to find it and say, "This is it." However, Prāsaṅgika
Mādhyamikas assert that although one searches in this way, one does not
find it. Therefore they say that the appearance of a phenomenon as existing
from its own side is a mistaken appearance.

If production of something such as a sprout were to exist from its own
side, production from one of the four alternatives would be found, but it is
not. Accordingly, Nāgārjuna says in the first verse of *Fundamental Verses on
the Middle Way*:

In no sense is anything
ever produced,
whether from itself, from other,
from both, or without a cause.

Therefore sprouts and so forth have no production that is ultimately
established or established from its own side. Similarly, Candrakīrti's *Entering the Middle Way* states (6.151):

A chariot is neither asserted to be other than its parts
nor to be non-other. It does not possess them.
It does not depend on the parts, and the parts do not
depend on it.
Neither is it the mere collection of the parts, nor is it
their shape. [Searching for the self] is like this.

Just as one cannot find a chariot by searching in these seven ways, one cannot find the self by searching in these seven ways. Therefore Candrakīrti indicates that, like the chariot, the self does not ultimately exist. Similarly, Nāgārjuna's *Precious Garland* states (1.80):

> The person is not earth, not water,
> not fire, not wind, not space,
> not consciousness, and not all of them.
> Yet what person is there apart from these?

As Nāgārjuna states, since one cannot find the person within its basis of imputation—form, consciousness, and so forth—or somewhere other than that, the person does not ultimately exist.

In the system of the essentialists, if a phenomenon exists it must exist from its own side, for if this phenomenon did not exist from its own side it would not exist at all. This is not true in the Prāsaṅgika Madhyamaka system. For example, in the Prāsaṅgika Madhyamaka system, by merely imputing with terms and concepts "This is Devadatta" in dependence on seeing Devadatta's aggregates, the mode of existence of Devadatta—the person who experiences happiness and suffering—is encompassed. Therefore they posit that Devadatta has the ability to perform functions by being merely imputed by conception.

From the perspective of essentialists, being merely imputed by conception does not encompass the mode of existence. They assert that, by searching for that which is Devadatta when you make the imputation "This is Devadatta," you must find Devadatta to exist from his own side so that you identify, "This is him." On investigation, if you do not find Devadatta, Devadatta would not exist from his own side, and therefore he would have to be completely and utterly nonexistent. From the perspective of a Prāsaṅgika Mādhyamika, essentialists who make such an assertion do not avoid asserting one of the two extremes—permanence or annihilation. When they assert that persons and so forth exist from their own side, they fall into the extreme of permanence. When they assert that persons capable of performing functions do not exist because they do not exist from their own side, they fall into the extreme of annihilation.

The master Candrakīrti states this in his *Commentary on the Four Hundred Stanzas*:

> Essentialists say that whenever things exist, they have an essence. As they see it, without essence these things would be completely nonexistent, like the horn of a donkey. Therefore these essentialists cannot avoid being proponents of both extremes of permanence and annihilation. Consequently, it is difficult to reconcile all of their explicit assertions.[88]

4. How Phenomena Exist

When You Search for the Imputed Object, You Do Not Find It

According to Nāgārjuna's *Fundamental Verses on the Middle Way* and Can-drakīrti's *Entering the Middle Way*, essentialists assert that the sensory faculties, consciousness, person, and so forth essentially exist, being produced and ceasing by their own essence. But if this were so, you would be able to analyze production, the person, and so forth with reasons that investigate reality—the four alternatives, the sevenfold analysis, and so forth—and find them very clearly and be able to say with certainty, "This is it." However, this is not what you discover after such an analysis. You discover only the lack of essential existence and the emptiness of inherent existence. In this vein, Candrakīrti's *Commentary on the Four Hundred Stanzas* states:

> When reason analyzes in this way, no essential nature is found existing in the sensory faculties, objects, or consciousnesses; hence, they have no essential existence. If they existed essentially, reasoned analysis would clarify their essential existence, but it does not. Therefore they are established as empty of intrinsic nature.[89]

For the Prāsaṅgikas, although eyes and so forth do not exist from their own side, they do exist in general. As explained above, you search with reasoning analyzing reality for existence by intrinsic nature—or from the side of phenomena. When you do not find this when searching for it in that way, this refutes phenomena existing by their own essential nature. But this does not refute the production and so on that is the dependent arising of the eyes and so on that are the fruit of karma. In this vein, the *Commentary on the Four Hundred Stanzas* states:

Because our analysis is intent on seeking intrinsic nature, we refute here that things exist essentially; we do not refute that eyes and such are products and are dependently arisen results of karma.[90]

Refuting Production via the Four Alternatives Does Not Refute Production Per Se

If things had production by their intrinsic nature, production from their own side, or ultimate production, they would have to have production from (1) themselves, (2) other, (3) both self and other, or (4) causelessly. These are the four alternatives introduced in the first verse of Nāgārjuna's treatise on the Middle Way, which was cited near the end of the last chapter. As things are not produced from any of those, ultimate production is refuted. Some extend this reasoning analyzing the ultimate to say that it also reveals an emptiness that refutes even the mere production of phenomena from causes and conditions. But if this were so, functional things would not be functional, as they would be empty of the ability to produce effects. For, like the son of a barren woman, they would be utterly nonexistent. As this would then lead to the dire extreme of nihilism, we should avoid this view. The production we are refuting is the production that seems to exist from its own side, which is how it ordinarily appears to us. It does not truly exist the way that it appears. Yet composite things perform functions and produce effects, just like a magician's illusions and so forth are able to produce effects. In this vein, the *Commentary on the Four Hundred Stanzas* states:

> *Claim*: Āryadeva means that compounded phenomena lack production because this analysis refutes all forms of production.
>
> *Reply*: In that case, the production of compounded phenomena would not be said to be like a magician's illusion. Rather, we would use examples such as the son of a barren woman to illustrate how production exists. Wary of the absurd implication that dependent arisings would not exist, we avoid such comparisons. Instead, we compare the production of things to a magician's illusion and so forth, examples that do not contradict dependent arising.[91]

The Ways of Conventions Are Not Feasible
if Posited after Analysis

Prāsaṅgikas such as the master Nāgārjuna posit presentations of the basis, path, and goal[92] without investigating with the reasoning analyzing the ultimate, whereas the essentialists posit them only after investigation with the reasoning analyzing the ultimate. But in the latter case, say the Prāsaṅgikas, you would have posited those phenomena as ultimately established or established in reality. And as we have seen, phenomena that are posited in this way cannot exist conventionally or nominally. For when you investigate with the reasoning analyzing the ultimate, you are unable to posit any phenomenon that exists in the conventions of the world, and these conventionally existent phenomena would then become nonexistent. As Candrakīrti states in his *Explanation of Entering the Middle Way*:

When you use analysis, the conventions of the world are destroyed. As it says in the sutras:

For instance, when the three come together—the moving hand and
the instrument's wood and strings—
they produce a sound
arising from the instrument—the lute, flute, and so on.

Then some scholars analyze this saying,
"From where does this come and to where does it go?"
When they investigate in all the cardinal and intermediate directions,
they do not find the coming or going of sound.[93]

Candrakīrti's *Clear Words* states:

Therefore the masters present it as being established from the perspective of existing by mere interdependence. We assert this without any doubt just as it is. Were it otherwise, either conventional phenomena would not be possible or they would be ultimately established but not conventionally existent.[94]

Establishing Phenomena Not through Analysis
but on the Basis of Mere Dependent Imputation

Those who propound existence from the object's side say that after you analyze phenomena that are causes or effects—chariots and so forth—they will be found to exist. Mādhyamikas who say that phenomena have no essence say that you can refute the notion of a chariot, for instance, existing in its own right through performing a sevenfold analysis. Essentialists then say to the Mādhyamikas: "If you refute a chariot's existence in its own right by searching in these seven ways, then conventional phenomena of the world—such as an opponent of the Middle Way buying a chariot or delivering a chariot—become impossible for you." In other words, essentialists accuse Mādhyamikas of nihilism because essentialists believe that to refute intrinsic existence is to refute existence altogether.

In response to the essentialists the Mādhyamikas say: This fault is true of you essentialists, not of us. How is this so? When you [essentialists] analyze any phenomenon that you posit, you search for it, find it, and posit things as established. You do not accept establishing a chariot by merely taking as its basis of imputation whatever parts appear, such as a chariot's wheels and so forth, and then saying, 'This is a chariot,' imputing a worldly convention without pursuing any analysis or investigation. Therefore the conventions of buying a chariot and so forth are impossible for you. For us Mādhyamikas, although the chariot does not exist in its own right, conventional objects such as chariots do not incur the fault of unfeasibility. When you analyze using the sevenfold analysis and so forth, a chariot is not established either conventionally or ultimately, but when you do not analyze and take as your basis of imputation whatever part appears, such as the wheels and so forth, and merely designate with terms and concepts, "This is a chariot," you can posit the existence of a functioning chariot.

In this vein, Candrakīrti states in his *Explanation of Entering the Middle Way*:

This fault is only true of you essentialists. It is like this: When one searches in the seven ways, as previously explained, a chariot is not feasible.[95] You posit a phenomenon as existent after analysis and do not assert any other way of establishment. Therefore how can you establish worldly conventions such as "bring the chariot"? The fault is not ours. How so?

This chariot is not established in the seven ways,
either in reality or for the world.
Yet without analysis, just for the world,
it is imputed in dependence on its parts.[96]

Also Candrakīrti's *Clear Words* states:

Worldly persons do not enter into analysis wherein they say such things as "from both self and other" and so forth but realize merely this: "This effect comes from this cause." The master [Nāgārjuna] also presented it in this way.[97]

REFUTING PHENOMENA EXISTING IN THEIR OWN RIGHT DOES NOT REFUTE PHENOMENA

The *Heart Sutra* states, "There is no form"[98] and so on, and the *Sutra of the Ultimate Emptiness* says, "Do not observe an agent." Mādhyamikas say that such refutations of the aggregates and of a person who is an agent of karmic actions are not refuting their conventional existence but their intrinsic existence, their existing in their own right, their ultimate existence, and their nature that is substantially existent in the sense of being self-sufficient. There does exist an agent of nonvirtuous and virtuous karmic actions that is a mere dependent imputation and an agent that is able to function in the sense of experiencing the effects of happiness and suffering; this agent is not refuted.

Candrakīrti quotes the *Sutra of the Ultimate Emptiness* in his *Explanation of Entering the Middle Way*:

Do not observe an agent from that.
Karma exists and maturation as well.[99]

You should understand from this statement the refutation of an intrinsically existent agent, but you should not think, "This also refutes its conventional component, its dependent imputation." This is echoed in the *Heart Sutra*, which states:

Correctly view even those five aggregates as empty of intrinsic existence.[100]

And the *Perfection of Wisdom in 100,000 Verses* states:

It is so by the power of worldly convention but not ultimately.[101]

WITH MERE DEPENDENT IMPUTATION, FUNCTIONALITY IS FEASIBLE

Just as explained above, in this Prāsaṅgika system when you apply the five-fold analysis of sameness, difference, and so forth to the basis of imputation of, for example, a pitcher—the bulbous portion, the spout, and so forth—you see that the pitcher does not exist. However, a proponent of the Prāsaṅgika system is able to posit by mere imputation on the basis of imputation—a bulbous portion and so forth—a pitcher that is able to perform the functions of holding and pouring water. Essentialists do not know how to posit this. This is said to be an amazing and exclusive feature of the Prāsaṅgika Madhyamaka system.

Candrakīrti states in his *Commentary on the Four Hundred Stanzas*:

A pitcher and so forth are not found to exist on application of the fivefold analysis to determine whether they are one with their "cause" [i.e., their basis of imputation] or other than their basis of imputation. Nonetheless, as dependent imputations, they are capable of such functions as holding and dispensing honey, water, milk, and so forth. How amazing is this![102]

DOES A VALID COGNITION OBSERVE CONVENTIONAL PHENOMENA?

From the *King of Concentration Sutra*:

The eye, ear, and nose consciousness are not valid cognizers. The tongue, body, and mental consciousnesses are also not valid cognizers.

If these sense consciousnesses were valid cognizers,
of what use to anyone would the noble beings' path be?[103]

Candrakīrti states in his *Entering the Middle Way* (6.31a), "The world is not valid in any way." Thus it is said that the physical sensory faculties (the eye and so forth) and the sensory consciousnesses of worldly persons (the visual consciousness and so forth) are not valid cognizers. Furthermore, Nāgārjuna states in the opening homage of his *Fundamental Verses on the Middle Way*:

I bow down to the perfect Buddha
the best of teachers, who taught that
whatever is dependently arisen is
unceasing, unborn,
unannihilated, not permanent,
not coming, not going,
without distinction, without identity,
and free from conceptual elaboration.

Assertion: The sublime wisdom of a noble being (*ārya*) in meditative equipoise does not see or take as its object conventional phenomena, which are the elaborations of production and cessation of dependently arisen phenomena. Thus conventional phenomena are not observed by either conventional valid cognition or valid cognition that observes the ultimate. Therefore these phenomena do not exist.

Response: In this Prāsaṅgika system, that which is called *valid cognition* is not mistaken in regard to its principal phenomenon—its object of engagement. In general, they also posit as valid cognition the ability to engage either a subtle or a coarse object. The physical sense faculties generally do not have the ability to engage subtle objects, and it is therefore said that they are unsuitable to be valid cognizers. Thus it is necessary to posit as a valid cognizer the *mind* that illuminates and knows its object. The *King of Concentration Sutra* states:

It is like this: these sensory faculties are not valid cognizers.
They are naturally material and ethically neutral.[104]

Dharmakīrti's *Commentary on Valid Cognition* states (2.3b–4c):

> Mind is the valid cognizer
> because it is the principal thing that engages
> objects to adopt or discard.
> Because there are different kinds of objects,
> they are cognized by different kinds of minds.
> Once this [undeceived mind] exists, this [ability to
>   have a continuum of valid cognitions] exists.

The statements from the sutra and from *Entering the Middle Way* above regarding the mind and the visual consciousness and so forth not being valid cognizers are not saying that these minds are not valid cognizers with respect to any object whatsoever. They are saying that these minds do not validly cognize the ontological status or reality of their objects or their objects' establishment by way of their own characteristics[105] or establishment in their own right. Living beings conceive phenomena—forms, sounds, and so forth—as being established by their own characteristics or from their own side. They appear to living beings to be findable even by a direct perception. But these objects are not true as they appear. Therefore they are called "truths for a concealer," "falsities," or "deceptions."
The *Descent to Laṅkā Sutra* states:

> These objects exist conventionally;
> ultimately they have no inherent existence.
> That which is mistaken with respect to the lack
>   of inherent existence
> is that which is a truth for a concealer.[106]

Living beings conceive such objects as form and so forth to be established in their own right, and these objects appear to exist in their own right to their visual and other sense consciousnesses. If these were to really exist in that way, then our consciousnesses would perceive forms and so forth in accord with their actual ontological status. In that case, these consciousnesses perceiving forms and so forth to exist in their own right or to be established by way of their own characteristics would necessarily be perceptions of what is true. Then forms and so forth existing in their own right would be the ontological status of composite things. Our sensory consciousnesses would then perceive the reality of form and so forth, and our sensory consciousnesses would necessarily be valid cognizers of the reality of forms, sounds, and the rest. Were this the case, then ordinary persons would have accurately perceived the ontological status of composite things from beginningless time and would have become accustomed to that. Therefore it would be senseless for them to seek the path of noble beings, who accurately know the ontological status of composite things. These ordinary beings would have already eliminated the afflictions and misconceptions with regard to the ontological status of phenomena and would not need to later appropriate composite things—that is, the aggregates of cyclic existence. Being liberated from cyclic existence, why would they not like it? As verse 3 of Nāgārjuna's *Sixty Stanzas of Reasoning* states:

If things were actually true
in accordance with ordinary persons' thought,
as they would have no things [no aggregates],
why would they not like their liberation?

As we saw above in the *King of Concentration Sutra*:

If these sense consciousnesses were valid cognitions,
of what use to anyone would the noble beings' path be?

Also Candrakīrti's *Entering the Middle Way* states:

If the [cognitions of] worldly persons were valid,
they would see reality, so what would be the necessity
    of the noble beings' paths?
What would be the use of their paths?
[The cognitions of] the foolish are not suitable
    to be valid.

His *Explanation of Entering the Middle Way* states:

If one asserts that the cognitions of the worldly are valid, and
that they see reality truly, then one must accept that they have

eliminated ignorance. For this reason, the cognitions of the foolish are not suitable to be valid.[107]

And also:

> If you say merely that the eyes and so forth ascertain reality, then there would be no need for diligent effort along with its effect with regard to ethical discipline, study, reflection, meditation, and so forth for the sake of cognizing the noble path. Therefore that is not true.[108]

Entering the Middle Way states (6.23):

> All things bear two natures
> found by correct and false views.
> The object of those who see correctly is said to be "reality,"
> and the object of those who see falsely is said to be "conventional truth."

Thus all phenomena in fact have two natures—ultimate and conventional. In terms of the apprehending consciousness, there are also accordingly two cognitions—valid cognition that realizes the conventional and valid cognition that realizes the ultimate. Moreover, as stated above, in this Prāsaṅgika system, valid cognition is posited as an awareness that is not deceived with respect to its principal object, its object of engagement. With respect to valid cognition, they uniquely assert four types: perceptual cognition, inferential cognition, analogy, and verbal testimony.[109] Je Tsongkhapa said that in brief these four can be included within two types of valid cognition—perceptual and inferential.

Also Candrakīrti said in his *Commentary on the Four Hundred Stanzas*:

> In the world an undeceived cognition is seen to be valid.[110]

Nāgārjuna's *Dispelling Debates* states:

> There are inferential, analogy, and verbal testimony valid cognitions—

inferential [proves a point with a correct reason], verbal
testimony with citation,
and analogy with an example.
[One can respond with these and] with a perceptual
valid cognition.[111]

Also Candrakīrti's *Clear Words* states:

One establishes the knowledge of a worldly meaning with the
four valid cognitions.[112]

As to the presentation of valid cognition and its cognized objects, this is
done with valid cognitions and cognized objects that exist by being merely
posited relative to each other and mutually dependent on each other. It is
not necessary for an object that is established by valid cognition to be established by way of its own essence. *Clear Words* states:

[Valid cognitions and their cognized objects] are established
through the force of mutual interdependence—by virtue of the
presence of valid cognition, there come to be cognized objects,
and by virtue of the presence of cognized objects, there come to
be valid cognitions. But there is no intrinsic establishment of
either the valid cognitions or the cognized objects.[113]

Take the example of a chariot. Although it is not established as a chariot by way of its essential nature, due to the appearance of any of its
parts—the wheels, the chassis, and so forth—to the visual consciousness
we apprehend it as a chariot. Also, our mental consciousness conceives as
a basis [of imputation] whatever appears to the visual consciousness and
from that imputes "This is a chariot," without analysis or examination as
to what among those parts is a chariot. This mere imputation suffices as
the way to establish a chariot that is able to perform the function of trans-
port. Therefore both the visual consciousness and mental consciousness
are posited as valid cognitions that are not deceived with respect to the
chariot.

How a Chariot Exists Conventionally

These undeceived cognitions engage their objects according to how they appear and are upheld in the conventions of the world. They engage their object, such as a chariot, without analyzing its ontological status, without dissatisfaction regarding that. Therefore they are called "cognitions that engage without analysis or investigation," "cognitions of worldly conventions," and "what is upheld by the world." Their objects, phenomena such as chariots, are said to exist "by the power of convention," "by mere conceptual imputation," and "by the power of conceptualization."

Question: Can you posit as existent whatever is upheld by the world and whatever is imputed by concept?

Answer: No, it is not like that. Although something may be upheld by the world, if it is undermined by reasoning, it is not suitable to be posited as existing even conventionally. For example, in the world one finds the apprehension of a self that is established by its essential nature and the apprehension of what belongs to that self. Also there is the apprehension of a prior mountain being the mountain of the present. Therefore, although these are upheld by the world, they do not exist in that way.

Question: What is the meaning of existing conventionally or not existing conventionally?

Answer: Je Tsongkhapa states in his *Great Treatise*:

> How does one determine whether something exists conventionally? We hold that something exists conventionally (1) if it is known to a conventional consciousness, (2) if no other conventional valid cognition contradicts its being as it is thus known, and (3) if reason that accurately analyzes reality—that is, analyzes whether something intrinsically exists—does not contradict it. We hold that what fails to meet those criteria does not exist.[114]

Question: Above you declared as your foundation the words of Je Tsongkhapa—his *Great Treatise's* section on insight—and then said that you will explain the existence of phenomena that are the products of dependent arising as able to perform their individual functions.[115] However, what you are explaining here is only citations of statements from the master

Candrakīrti's *Clear Words*, his commentary on the *Four Hundred Stanzas*, and so forth. One does not see any explanation of any stages of the path texts. Why did you not explain any of Tsongkhapa's unique assertions?

Answer: What you say is true. Je Tsongkhapa specially selected some important points that exist in the words of the master Nāgārjuna and his disciples that did not catch the attention of many great scholars, and he explained these points. In doing so, he neither created any new terminology for the conventions in the treatises of those masters nor changed the meaning of their words.

What especially stands out in the minds of those who analyze this clearly? These phenomena—pitchers and so on—are empty of being established from their own side or of being ultimately established. However, conventionally you posit their existence, which is established by valid cognition as being able to perform their individual functions. Those who single-mindedly think that these and other points in the texts of Je Tsongkhapa's works are new assertions that are not in accord with those of the father Ārya Nāgārjuna and his sons might engage in provocative critique, thinking, "How can this be?" Even though there may be only a few who think this way, I thought it nonetheless valuable to show how all these ideas are grounded in the treatises of Candrakīrti and the like and explain these a little.

5. The Trainings of the Three Types of Persons

Regarding what practices are necessary to engage in at the outset, the crucial teachings that the Blessed One gave to his disciples are as follows: the cause that brings suffering to you and others, in this life and in futures lives, by producing a very miserable rebirth as a hell being, hungry ghost, or an animal is the ten nonvirtuous deeds—killing, stealing, and so on. Therefore the Buddha advised that you must abstain from these. The perfect cause that results in rebirth in the high states of humans and gods is ethical discipline of abstaining from the ten nonvirtuous deeds and the cultivation of the ten virtuous deeds that are their opposite—protecting life, generosity, and so forth. Therefore the Buddha said that you must practice these. The *Perfect Renunciation Sutra* states:

> In the beginning, the blessed buddhas teach generosity, the teaching of ethical discipline, the teaching of the high states of humans and gods . . .[116]

Nāgārjuna's *Precious Garland* (5.38) states:

> From generosity comes wealth, from ethical discipline happiness,
> from patience beauty, from virtuous effort brilliance,
> from meditative stabilization peace, and from wisdom liberation.
> From compassion all aims are achieved.

In this way, the Buddha's disciples properly practiced the teachings leading to higher birth from the outset. Without mixing your physical, verbal, and mental activities with harm to others, you must become able to naturally strive at the ten virtuous deeds that benefit others.

ESSENTIAL TEACHINGS FOR THE MIDDLE: THE TEACHINGS ON THE DEFINITE GOODNESS OF LIBERATION

When those disciples firmly establish a basis of ethical discipline that abandons nonvirtuous deeds, become free from the obscurations of ill deeds, and automatically make virtuous effort with enthusiasm, they see that they are able to avoid birth into miserable realms in their future lives and to obtain the high state of a happy rebirth among humans and gods. Although they are able to attain this, it is not a permanent freedom from miserable rebirths. Moreover, the higher birth of humans and gods does not transcend the nature of suffering. Therefore their minds turn toward liberation, thinking, "Am I able to liberate myself from suffering completely and forever?" When this happens they become the fortunate disciples of the foremost teaching, the teaching of the four noble truths. The *Perfect Renunciation Sutra* states:

> When the blessed ones see a joyful mind, a satisfied mind, a mind that is free of obscurations, that dwells in good fortune and has an ability to comprehend their explanations of the foremost teaching, then the buddhas, the blessed ones, will explain the foremost teaching. What is the foremost teaching that they explain in detail? It is the four noble truths: true sufferings, true origins, true cessations, and true paths.[117]

ESSENTIAL TEACHINGS FOR THE END: THE TEACHINGS ON THE HIGHEST DEFINITE GOODNESS OF OMNISCIENCE

The method of attaining the highest definite goodness of omniscience is as follows: when, in the beginning, you train your mind in the paths of the persons of beginning and middle capacities as stated above, you consider, through the twelve factors of dependent arising, how one enters cyclic existence and how one ends cyclic existence, and through this, generate the attitude of the determination to be free from cyclic existence and the uncontrived mind that desires liberation from it. Likewise, when training your mind in the path of the person of greatest capacity, you contemplate how other beings, like yourself, enter into cyclic existence through the twelve factors of dependent arising and how they end cyclic existence. From this contemplation, you understand your own and others' births in cyclic existence as being beginningless and without number.

Then you comprehend that over the course of previous lives, all other living beings have been your dear parents, like your dear parents of this lifetime. Recognizing all beings as your mother, you recall that when acting as your mother, they were so kind, just like your mother of this lifetime. You then wish to repay their kindness, just as you do your mother of this lifetime. Becoming repeatedly accustomed to these three ways of thinking, you come to have the love that feels affection for all other living beings, just as you would your own mother of this life.

Furthermore, you think over, repeatedly, how you are equal to others in wanting happiness and not wanting suffering; how problematic it has been that, from beginningless time up to now, you have held on to the idea of cherishing yourself and have engaged in ways of thinking that neglect other living beings; and how beneficial it is that the buddhas and bodhisattvas, for the sake of others, disregard themselves and cherish others as they would themselves. Becoming accustomed to these thoughts, you produce the attitude of exchanging self and other by forgetting about yourself as you usually forget about others and by cherishing others as you cherish yourself.

After you have, in this way, become endowed with a loving mind for all beings, you contemplate how these beings enter cyclic existence through the twelve factors of dependent arising and how they could reverse that process. Once you do this, just as you cannot bear being tormented by the sufferings of cyclic existence in this way, so you cannot endure others being tormented in this way. You then produce the great compassion that wants to free them from their suffering. Then you generate the spirit of enlightenment that wants to attain the high state of a buddha, who has eliminated all faults and completed all good qualities stemming from eliminating what is to be eliminated and realizing all that is to be realized, for the sake of your being able to free all living beings from their suffering. In order to do this you must practice the six perfections—the deeds of the bodhisattvas, who are the heirs of the buddhas—for eons. This is the teaching for the person of great capacity, the teaching you must train in at the end.

6. Escaping the Wheel of Life

ORIGINS OF THE WHEEL OF LIFE

The Buddha taught in the *Exegesis of the Discipline* that his disciples Śāriputra and Maudgalyāyana both traveled throughout the world of the hell beings, hungry ghosts, animals, gods, and humans and directly saw their suffering.[118] After they returned to this world of Jampudvīpa, they described what they had seen to the four types of listeners—monks, nuns, laymen, and laywomen. They talked about the hell beings' suffering of having their bodies chopped, cut, and so forth; the hungry ghosts' suffering of hunger, thirst, and so on; the animals' suffering of eating one another; the gods' suffering at the time of their death and transition and their suffering of knowing that they will fall to the miserable realms; the humans' suffering of searching for resources, having attachment, and so forth. The people with whom they spoke who had previously spurned virtuous deeds came to appreciate them and have faith in them. Whenever both Śāriputra and Maudgalyāyana gave teachings in this way, a multitude of listeners gathered. Many people became followers of both Śāriputra and Maudgalyāyana, who gave them the teachings.

A great number of those who listened to Śāriputra and Maudgalyāyana's teachings discussed them, and word reached the Buddha, who said the following to Ānanda, "Such Dharma teachers as the monks Śāriputra and Maudgalyāyana will not exist in all times and in all places. Therefore, in the entryway to the Sangha's temples, my followers must draw a five-sectioned wheel of life with symbolic representations of the five types of beings. Then the Sangha must appoint a learned monk who is able to precisely teach the householders and brahmans who come to the temple the symbolic meaning of the wheel of life, the entry to and reversal of cyclic existence in terms of the four noble truths—the way beings enter cyclic existence by means of the twelve factors of dependent arising and the way to reverse that."

Just as the Teacher instructed, in ancient times there developed a custom of drawing a wheel of life in the entryway of the Sangha's temples. Even today, there is still a remaining example of this: a drawing of the wheel of life from the fifth century in the entryway of cave 17 at Ajanta. In 1968, I had an opportunity to see this when I stayed in that region of India and visited that cave. I wanted to determine what kind of drawing it was among the several different ways of drawing the sections of the wheel of life, but the conditions to view it clearly from up close were not available. Nevertheless, through an interested traveler who later went there at my request, I was able to see photos of that drawing. Because the drawings in that cave have been there for so many years, they had degenerated, and the wheel of life was not clearly discernable.

Although, in dependence on the Indian custom, there is this widespread tradition of including a drawing the wheel of life in the entryways of the Tibetan monastic temples, the custom of appointing a learned monk from the Sangha to explain to temple visitors the teaching from the viewpoint of the meaning of the symbolism in this picture did not, for the most part, spread.

The Symbols and Meanings of the Drawing of the Wheel of Life

In the center of the wheel of life is a drawing of a pig, an animal that signifies ignorance; issuing from its mouth are both a poisonous snake, which signifies hostility, and a pigeon, which signifies attachment. These three mental poisons are the root cause determining the environs and bodies of the five types of living beings within cyclic existence. In addition, both attachment and hostility are shown to be emerging from their root, ignorance.

Around this center are two pathways, white and black, which symbolize the experience of beings in the intermediate state. Living beings accumulate karma by the influence of any of the three mental poisons. Virtuous karma that results in rebirth in cyclic existence is motivated by the two poisons of ignorance and attachment to self. Nonvirtuous karma is motivated by all three mental poisons. In the drawing, the people moving upward on a white path symbolize how, at the time of being reborn in the happy realms of humans and gods due to the virtuous karma of abstaining from the ten nonvirtuous karmic actions, the beings of the intermediate state have an experience of going upward guided by a white light like that of the moon. Those intermediate-state beings destined for the hell, hungry ghost, or animal realms, due to the ten nonvirtuous karmic actions, experience going downward in darkness. The beings depicted here are being led by frightful hell demons.

Around this, in an image divided into five sections, are drawings of five different kinds of beings, the living beings who are the animate inhabitants that use the inanimate worldly habitat that is for their use. When you pass through cyclic existence due to karma and the afflictions, you do so as one of these five types of beings—hell beings, hungry ghosts, animals, humans, and gods—or six types when you divide the gods into gods and demigods. These sections also illustrate how as one of these beings you experience the suffering of pain, the suffering of change, and the suffering of pervasive conditioning.

The drawings in the ring of twelve images surrounding the five realms illustrate how the living beings of various types are born, transit to other lives, and after transitioning, take rebirth. This illustrates how a permanent, self-existent creator deity does not make them cycle; rather, living beings cycle due to their own karma and afflictions, passing through cyclic existence by means of the twelve factors of dependent arising:

1. The first image is a blind, old woman leaning on a walking stick. This illustrates the initial *ignorance* of not knowing precisely the nature of the self, thinking "I." Apprehending an independent "I" and an independent "mine," this ignorance acts as a motivating force for the karma that projects a birth as one of the five types of beings.

2. The second image is a potter creating a variety of pots. This illustrates the second factor of dependent arising of *conditioning factors*, or compositional activity, which has to do with our karma. The power of the ignorance that apprehends a self plants certain karmic predispositions in the consciousness. These conditioning factors project rebirth in cyclic existences that are either favorable or unfavorable.

3. The third image is of a monkey climbing in a tree. This illustrates the third factor of dependent arising, *consciousness*. Consciousness

holds the "potencies" or karmic predispositions of virtuous and nonvirtuous karma that project rebirths in cyclic existence, and it is what makes the connection to the next lifetime.

4. The fourth image depicts getting into a boat. This illustrates the varieties of *name-and-form*. *Form* here is the combination of semen and ovum (which is dependent on the consciousness) until its transformation into the sense faculties of the eye, ear, nose, and tongue. *Name* is the consciousness that resides with the aggregate of form, its concomitant mental processes of discrimination and feelings, and the compositional factors. This fourth image illustrates any combination of name-and-form, the aggregates that are a karmic ripening at the moment when the birth stage[119] occurs.

5. The fifth image is an empty house. This illustrates the fifth factor of dependent arising, the *six sense-bases*. This is the newly formed sensory faculties—visual, auditory, and so on—which are the aggregates that are a karmic ripening during the existence stage, which is previous to death.

6. The sixth image depicts kissing a child, which illustrates the sixth factor of dependent arising, *contact*. Contact is a mental factor that, once the object, sensory faculty, and consciousness newly come together, distinguishes the attributes of the object.

7. The seventh image is a person whose eye is being pierced by an arrow. This illustrates the seventh factor of dependent arising, *feeling*. The condition of contact, which arises from the assembly of the object, sensory faculty, and consciousness, causes an experience of pleasure or pain to arise in the mind, predominantly experienced as a feeling.

8. The eighth image is a person drinking beer, which illustrates the eighth factor of dependent arising, *craving*. This is a craving for pleasure and freedom from pain, which further makes potent the karma that projects future rebirth.

9. The ninth image is of a person picking fruit from a tree, which illustrates the ninth factor of dependent arising, *grasping*. This is a form of attachment, an excessive craving for the resources of existence for the sake of obtaining them.

10. The tenth image is a pregnant woman, which illustrates the tenth factor of dependent arising, *becoming*. Craving and grasping nurture the karma of the previous second factor, conditioning factors. This karma now becomes potent and can project the next rebirth. Calling this karma "the tenth factor, becoming" is a case of giving the name of the effect, becoming (i.e., cyclic existence), to the cause.

11. The eleventh image is a woman giving birth to an infant, which illustrates the eleventh factor of dependent arising, *birth*. This is the birth stage of the next lifetime, a rebirth arisen from and connected to the karma called *becoming*.

12. The twelfth image is an undertaker carrying a human corpse, which illustrates the twelfth factor of dependent arising, *aging and death*. *Aging* is the transformation of the physical state of the being you have been born as in the above rebirth. *Death* occurs when that aging being sheds his or her respective aggregates.

The Kadam *Father Teachings* states:

"If I were to ask you to illustrate these twelve factors, what, O conqueror, would you say they are like?"

The teacher [Atiśa] taught [Drom] the following.
This is taught in scripture:
ignorance is like a blind old woman,
conditioning factors resemble a potter,
while consciousness is like a monkey,
name-and-form is like getting into a boat,
while the six sense-bases are like an empty region,
contact is said to be "like a kiss,"
while feeling is like an arrow in the eye,
craving is said to be "like drinking beer,"
while grasping is like reaching for fruit,
becoming is said to be "like a pregnant woman,"
while birth is like birthing that child,
aging and death is said to be "like carrying a corpse."[120]

The lord of death, Yama, is grabbing the outside of the wheel of cyclic existence and devouring it.[121] This drawing illustrates that all the habitats and inhabitants of cyclic existence are impermanent in the sense of being under the sway of karma and the afflictions. They do not pass beyond the nature of perishing; all must ultimately be consumed by their impermanence.

Elevated above and distinct from that wheel of life, without being mixed with it, the Blessed Buddha, the Teacher, is depicted, standing with his arm extended and pointing at the full moon, which symbolizes nirvana. This illustration external to the central picture symbolizes the truth of the path—the method of being liberated from cyclic existence—and the truth of the cessation that is complete liberation from cyclic existence and its causes, symbolized by a white moon in the sky.

Any teaching of the Buddha is only for the sake of his followers' temporarily obtaining higher rebirth—the high state of a human or a god—and ultimately obtaining the definite goodness of liberation and omniscience. Furthermore, you must accomplish these by contemplating the way we enter cyclic existence and the way we end that process in terms of the twelve factors of dependent arising.

The method to do this is as follows: In the beginning, as the means of attaining higher rebirth, you contemplate how happiness and suffering are effects that arise from virtuous and nonvirtuous karmic actions, and how, through the influence of ignorance, you accumulate nonvirtuous karmic actions and then pass through cyclic existences as hell beings, hungry ghosts, and animals. Contemplating this, you desire freedom from this process. To attain this freedom, you acquire a correct worldly view, which is understanding with conviction that happiness and suffering arise from virtuous and nonvirtuous karmic actions, respectively. You then contemplate the stages of cessation—the cessation of the ignorance that is confused about cause and effect and so forth. You thereby abstain from the ten nonvirtuous karmic actions, harming others, and learn properly the ten virtuous karmic actions, through which you help others. In this manner, you attain higher rebirth, the high state of a human or a god.

Furthermore, to obtain nirvana, the complete liberation from cyclic existence—freedom not only from rebirth in the miserable realms but also from rebirth in the happy realms of humans and gods—you contemplate how you cycle through rebirths as the six types of living beings by means of the six causal factors of dependent arising that are the true origins of suffering and the six effect factors of dependent arising that are true sufferings. Reflecting on the methods for cultivating the true cessations that end that process and the path that is the means of ending that process, you obtain the definite goodness of liberation by training in the eightfold noble path and so forth.

Therefore the excellent and peerless method to generate the thought of renunciation of cyclic existence entails reflecting on the forward and reverse orders of the afflictive factors of dependent arising. And the superior and peerless method for generating a genuine uncontrived intention for liberation involves contemplating the forward and reverse orders of the pure factors of dependent arising.

Again, with regard to the drawing of the wheel of life, it is said that the Buddha gave instructions to write below the wheel of life two verses, as explained in *Exegesis of the Discipline*:

> Undertaking this and leaving that,
> enter into the teaching of the Buddha.
> Like an elephant in a thatched house,
> destroy the forces of the lord of death.

> Those who with thorough conscientiousness
> practice this disciplined doctrine
> will forsake the wheel of birth,
> bringing sufferings to an end.[122]

This scripture also explains how to contemplate conditioning factors—the second factor of dependent arising, which projects rebirth in cyclic existences as the five or six types of beings due to the initial ignorance apprehending a self. This contemplation then continues up to how aging and death arises depending on the eleventh factor of dependent arising, birth. The scripture explains this contemplation of how you pass through cyclic existence, from beginningless time up to now, under the power of causal karma and afflictions in terms of this forward order. Furthermore, it explains how to contemplate the way to end initial ignorance by meditating on its countermeasure, the truth of the path that directly knows the nonexistence of the self that is the referent object of ignorance. Due to the cessation of ignorance, the second factor, conditioning factors, ceases. This process of cessation continues until due to the cessation of birth, aging and death cease. You should *undertake*[123] joyous perseverance with respect to the cessation of cyclic existence by means of the reverse order. You will certainly emerge from cyclic existence, *leaving* behind attachment to and clinging to the marvels of cyclic existence. In this way you *enter* the purpose of the verbal *teaching of the Buddha*—the adopting and discarding described within the four noble truths, the way of cause and effect for entering cyclic existence and reversing that process.

Moreover, just *like an elephant* destroying *a thatched house*, those who are intent on liberation destroy the afflictions of craving and so forth, *the forces of the lord of death*. After becoming *thoroughly conscientious*, they will practice *this disciplined doctrine* of the eightfold noble path that disciplines the afflictions—the wisdom that directly knows selflessness and so forth. They will then eliminate *birth* in cyclic existence and sever the continuity of the *sufferings* of birth, aging, sickness, death, and so forth.

In every single statement of the Buddha's teaching concerning the basis, path, and goal, he makes dependent arising the fundamental basis. When arriving at the final conclusion, his essential points are about dependent arising. While dependently arisen phenomena are empty of inherent establishment, all activities and functions are feasible as dependent arisings. Realizing that this is very difficult to understand, our Teacher, after reaching completely perfect buddhahood in Bodhgaya, stayed without giving the teaching about freedom from elaborations for seven weeks.

The Buddha directly saw the emptiness of inherent existence by means of the key point that phenomena are dependent arisings. Because he then taught it to others in that way, the Buddha is the peerless Teacher and the peerless Knower among all others who are called "teacher." The verbal teachings that reveal dependent arising are the quintessence of the verbal teachings, and the wisdom that realizes it is the quintessence of the realized teachings.

Though there are many avenues of praising Buddha in general, the glorious protector Ārya Nāgārjuna, considering such critical points in his most important works on Madhyamaka—*Fundamental Verses on the Middle Way*, *Sixty Stanzas of Reasoning*, *Dispelling Debates*, and *Praise of the Inconceivable*—praised the Buddha from the viewpoint of his teaching emptiness of inherent existence as the meaning of dependent arising. In the opening verse of his *Praise of Dependent Arising*, Je Tsongkhapa also praised the Buddha from the viewpoint of his teachings on dependent arising:

> He who speaks on the basis of seeing
> this makes him a knower and teacher unexcelled.
> I bow to you, O Conqueror, you who saw
> dependent arising and taught it.

Therefore phenomena's arising in dependence on causes and conditions, or on the basis of imputation and imputed terms and concepts, is like a kingpost for all Buddhist tenets and philosophical views.

The Greatness of the *Dependent Arising Sutra*[124]

The noble Mahayana sutra called *Dependent Arising* states:

> The phenomena that arise from causes,
> the Tathāgata proclaimed those causes
> as well as their cessation.
> Thus taught the Paragon of Virtue.[125]

This verse, the essence of the *Dependent Arising Sutra*, is renowned as the *Precious Treasure of the Buddha's Speech, the Sutra That Forms the Essence of Quintessential Dependent Arising and of the Profound Meaning of Emptiness and Then Teaches It.* This sutra reveals phenomena to be dependent arisings. For the disciples to whom it is taught, the fact that phenomena are dependent arisings takes on the meaning of being empty of existence from their own side. Based on this, the sutra reveals emptiness, the sphere of reality (*dharmadhātu*), and from this viewpoint, this sutra is also said to be called the *Sutra on the Sphere of Reality.*

By seeing dependent arising in dependence on this sutra, you attain two embodiments of a buddha. The first is the *nature embodiment (svabhāvika-kāya)*, which has two types: (1) the naturally pure sphere of reality of the mind, which is free of characteristics of true establishment, and (2) the mind that has been purified of all the adventitious defilements (the afflictive and cognitive obscurations). Second is the *sublime wisdom truth embodiment* (*jñānadharmakāya*), which knows all there is to know—impermanence, suffering, emptiness, selflessness, and so forth. The Sage actualized this truth embodiment. From this, his principal act for the benefit of others is this *Dependent Arising Sutra*, which fully comprises his thought. He presented it as the main object for his disciples to practice. Thus this *Dependent Arising Sutra* is also renowned as the "relic" of the Buddha's truth embodiment. He taught that proper practice of the meaning of this sutra in that way is the primary cause of ultimately obtaining quickly the truth embodiment of a tathāgata. The noble *Dependent Arising Sutra* states:

This dependent arising is the truth embodiment of the tathāgatas. Whoever sees dependent arising sees the Tathāgata.[126]

At the Pāṇḍukambala stone slab, a throne for the gods from the Heaven of the Thirty-Three Gods, Buddha gave this *Dependent Arising Sutra* to an assembly of śrāvakas, such as the noble Aśvajit, who was among the Buddha's first five disciples; bodhisattvas, such as the noble Maitreya; and a group of gods, including Brahmā, ruler of the beings of this Tolerable World,[127] Indra, the chief of the gods, and others. Furthermore, at the outset the noble Avalokiteśvara bowed respectfully to the Teacher, put his upper robe over his left shoulder, and requested, "In order to fulfill the wishes of those gods here who want to attain a very great effect from building a stupa, please teach them the Dharma and explain how to greatly increase merit and, in this world of gods, Māra, Brahmā, mendicants, and brahmans, explain how monks and nuns and male and female lay followers can maximize their merit." According to the noble *Dependent Arising Sutra*, the Teacher thereupon spoke the central stanza of the sutra.

Thus, if you construct a stupa and make this *Dependent Arising Sutra* one of the sacred objects that you place therein, you create very great merit. For example, even if some humans and gods were to make a stupa that was merely the size of a myrobalan fruit, place within it a kingpost merely the size of a pin, and make an umbrella for it with a mere *vakula* flower, they would generate the merit of Brahmā and then be reborn in the Brahmā worlds at the time of their deaths. Passing from there, they would then be born among the gods of the pure abodes.[128] This is stated in the noble *Dependent Arising Sutra*.

Dating back to former times in India, the land of the noble beings, there is an example of this custom of building a stupa and placing within it this *Dependent Arising Sutra*. An example is the great stupa known as the Dhamek Stupa in Sarnath, the town on the outskirts of Varanasi where I live. Even nowadays it remains a holy destination and object of offerings for Buddhist pilgrims. This stupa was built around 300 BCE during the reign of the Dharma king Aśoka.[129] When the British ruled India, they opened this stupa to see what was inside. Although they did not find therein any physical relics of the Buddha, it is said that inside on a stone slab ninety-one centimeters below the top of the stupa, they found a sixth- or seventh-century inscription of this *Dependent Arising Sutra* that reads:

Ye dharmā hetu prabhavā hetun teṣan tathāgato hyavadat
Teṣañ ca yo nirodha evaṃ vādī mahāśramaṇaḥ[130]

The phenomena that arise from causes,
the Tathāgata proclaimed those causes
as well as their cessation.
Thus taught the Paragon of Virtue.

There are five renditions of this sutra in the Tibetan canon.

Also, when the site of the glorious Nālandā Monastery's temple and stupa ruins was excavated, the British discovered many small clay tablets inscribed with this *Dependent Arising Sutra* as well as many similar figurines of Maitreya and Mañjuśrī. According to *Nalanda: Past and Present*, a collection of lectures during a seminar of scholars commemorating the twenty-fifth anniversary of a school at Nālandā, "In former times there was a custom of giving such figurines to faithful visitors to the temple."[131]

I have included these descriptions here to clarify that the custom of making this *Dependent Arising Sutra* a sacred object for inclusion when building a stupa, just as instructed in the sutra, dates back to ancient times.

Question: If this verse that begins with the line "The phenomena ..." is the spoken word of the Teacher, then because it also contains the phrases "the Tathāgata proclaimed" and "the Paragon of Virtue," the Teacher would be praising himself. Therefore this verse is not suitable to be the Teacher's spoken words.

Response: The Teacher Buddha has the qualities of the four fearlessnesses. He also praised himself in the *Perfect Renunciation Sutra*:

> There is no one like me.
> I have no master.
> In the world I am the one Buddha.
> I have attained genuine enlightenment.
>
> I outshine all; I know the entire world.
> I am not sullied by anything.
> Having eliminated all faults, become liberated, and free
>   of attachment,
> I have superknowledge. Who else would you depend upon?[132]

As he possessed the quality of fearlessness of assertion, he expressed his own greatness.

Also, the Teacher gave the teaching by means of the four fearlessnesses in the instance of this verse that begins with "The phenomena . . ."[133] By saying "The phenomena that arise from causes," the Buddha indicated that each of the phenomena that are the twelve factors of dependent arising comes into existence in dependence on the former factor acting as its cause, from conditioning factors [karma] arising in dependence on ignorance up to aging and death arising in the dependence on birth. Alternatively, he was indicating that all the phenomena that can be summarized as true sufferings—the dependent arising factors of birth, name-and-form, contact, feeling, aging and death, and so on—arise from the causes that are the dependent arising factors of initial ignorance, conditioning factors, consciousness, craving, grasping, becoming, and so forth. Hence, he is indicating that true sufferings arise from their causes, true origins—karma and the afflictions.

In short, with this first line of the verse the Buddha is saying, "The obstructions to liberation, or the cause of passing through cyclic existence by means of the twelve factors of dependent arising, is the afflictions that motivate karma. Those who desire liberation should not be involved with these." In asserting, "These are the obstructions," he gave the teaching in this line of the verse with one of the four fearlessnesses, the fearlessness of giving the teaching on obstructions.

With the second line, "the Tathāgata proclaimed those causes," the Buddha is saying, "These twelve factors—ignorance and so forth—have a cause that has a countermeasure that ceases karma and afflictions, which are the cause of cyclic existence, or the cause that is to be ceased. This countermeasure is the truth of the path, the direct perception of the selflessness of persons and objects. Therefore you must cultivate it." He gave this teaching by asserting definite emergence from the causes of cyclic existence, which, among the four fearlessnesses, is the fearlessness of indicating the path of definite emergence.

With the third line, "as well as their cessation," the Buddha is saying, "Relying on cultivating true paths directly cognizing the selflessness of persons and objects, which are the countermeasure to the afflictions, you will attain a cessation that brings an end to the suffering of cyclic existence and its causes. Thus the Buddha himself meditated in this way and eliminated suffering and its causes." The Buddha gave this teaching by means of the fearlessness of asserting his own aim of perfect abandonment.

With the fourth line, "Thus taught the Paragon of Virtue," the Buddha is saying, "The Teacher, the Paragon of Virtue, himself actualized true cessations and true paths in this way and brought to perfection the direct perception of what to adopt and what to abandon. As he taught accordingly, he is the Paragon of Virtue, or the Great Ascetic (*mahāśramaṇa*)." He gave this teaching by means of the fearlessness of asserting his own perfect realization.

In this way, the Teacher Buddha possesses the good qualities of the four fearlessnesses and thus had no sense of unease in asserting his own and others' aims when among his disciples. Therefore, when he called himself Tathāgata and Paragon of Virtue, he was showing "fearlessness." Maitreya's *Ornament of the Sutras* states (21.52):

You who teach the sublime wisdom, the abandonment
and the obstructions, and the definite emergence
required for both one's own and others' aims
are never disturbed by non-Buddhist philosophers.
Homage to you!

Maitreya's *Sublime Continuum* states (3.32):

Fearless like a lion among his disciples.

Furthermore, the Buddha had a purpose in stating the teachings with the four fearlessnesses. The Teacher knew the obstructions and the method for eliminating them. As he then accordingly engaged in adopting and abandoning, he acquired the good qualities of perfecting abandonment and realization. Because he thus had these good qualities, he taught them and asserted them to others. Thereby his disciples have exceeding faith and belief, and they also engage in adopting and abandoning.

In short, this stanza of four lines, "The phenomena that arise from causes..." and so on, indicates the basis of nirvana and cyclic existence, the four noble truths; the basis of method and wisdom, the two truths; the eightfold noble path, both method and wisdom; the goal of that, the truth embodiment (*dharmakāya*) that is the perfection of abandonment and realization; and the form embodiment (*rūpakāya*) possessing the four fearlessnesses. In addition, it refutes the nihilistic view that sees: the phenomena of cyclic existence and nirvana as having no cause; a permanent entity called "time" as the nonconcordant cause of those phenomena; and the way of things arising from a principal nature, a divine creator of the world, and so on. Integrating the ways of correctly positing the tenets of our own system into the way of dependent arising, it gives a condensed presentation in just four lines.

Therefore this *Dependent Arising Sutra*, being an important scripture that reveals great meaning in a few words, captures the Buddhist view and conduct at the basis, path, and goal levels. We must always recite this sutra, and by reflecting on its meaning, we must always treasure it as a writing about practice. We must understand that to do so is extremely important.

How You Enter into and Then
End Cyclic Existence

In the contemplation on how you enter into and end cyclic existence, you first contemplate how you pass through cyclic existence and then come to understand the basis, or root, from which birth and death and all the sufferings of cyclic existence arise. Once you understand the way to end the basis from which such sufferings arise, you strive to end cyclic existence by ending its causes; you cannot cast aside the suffering of cyclic existence like you remove a thorn from your flesh. For beings in cyclic existence, the basis for experiencing happiness or suffering is the various pleasant and fraught destinations, bodies, and resources for each of the six types of births. In connection with these, beings experience any of the three types of suffering[134] and continue to be born and die, cycling among the various realms of existence.

According to non-Buddhist systems, the cause—the root and basis from which this cyclic existence originates—is the principal nature, or a self-existent divine creator of the world, or the permanent and functioning being,[135] and so forth; all of these are unchanging, permanent, and enduring. If, in connection with the former and later moments of the mental continuum of a living being who is wandering in cyclic existence, this root cause is permanent and unchanging and remains without ceasing, then just as the living being is passing through cyclic existence now, he or she must pass through there also in the future without end. How can one be liberated from that? For as the cause cannot cease, it would likewise be impossible for the effect, cyclic existence, to cease. Dharmakīrti's *Commentary on Valid Cognition* states (2.134cd):

> Why does the cause abide?
> Because you do not see an end to the effect.

Question: What are the principal causes or seeds from which this cyclic existence arises, and who carries these seed-like causes?

Answer: Another person cannot drag you into cyclic existence. Since cyclic existence is something that beings experience, it must have a cause. And that cause must exist in connection with the former and present mental continuum of you, the being who is traversing cyclic existence. In general, a cause for perpetuating cyclic existence must be very powerful, fully manifest in yourself and others. And it cannot exist elsewhere than in your thoughts, your body, and your speech. Let's look at how this works.

Between your body and mind, your mind mistakenly has a view of "I" and "mine," and this gives rise to attachment and hostility. These make you crave to eliminate what you do not want and to acquire what you do want. To do that the mind then engenders actions of body and speech. These physical and verbal deeds can be either virtuous or nonvirtuous. Like this, you accumulate physical, verbal, and mental karma, both virtuous and nonvirtuous, over many lifetimes, and this karma along with the afflictions (*kleśa*) that fuel it are the principal causes of the happiness and suffering of cyclic existence. Another cause unconnected with these is impossible!

The glorious Dharmakīrti's *Commentary on Valid Cognition* states (2.81b–82a):

> Not led by some other living being,
> you try to rid yourself of suffering and attain happiness
> through attachment to your self.
> By this you take birth in this inferior place [cyclic existence].

Take as an illustration the way you experience happiness and suffering due to your thoughts and actions each day in this life, and through this understand other lifetimes as well. The way to do this is as follows. Continuously in your mindstream there is a mind that observes your self. This instinctual mind thinks "I," taking that "I" to exist as an independent thing, one not merely imputed to the collection of the mind and body or to either of them individually. Your apprehension of "I" considers the self to be independent.

If you pay attention to how this "I" mind views the self, how the self appears to this mind, and you deepen your investigation, you will be able to identify this mind that apprehends an independent "I," or self, more clearly. On the basis of this "I" mind, you become excessively attached to the self. And attachment to self triggers attachment to what belongs to the self— the things that bring you pleasure, your family and friends, and your possessions and wealth. You also become hostile toward things that threaten it.

Moreover, this "self" and "other" are like the near and far mountain: distinguished by perspective, they are only "self" and "other" relative to one another. There is no inherently established "self" and "other," no "self" or "other" defined by its own essence. Nevertheless, having set "self" apart from "other" by projecting an essence onto them, you generate a bias. You distinguish similarity or dissimilarity between households, districts, countries, races, religious views, political views, and so forth. Generally, you are attached to those things you associate with your self and hostile toward things associated with others. Due to this discrimination, the afflictions intensify, and your mind falls under their control. All the faults of cyclic existence in this and future lives arise from immersion in this dynamic.

Once your mind comes under the control of attachment and hostility, you think about eliminating the unwanted and acquiring the desired. You generate various intentions—the mental karma of intention—and this engenders physical and verbal actions. You then accumulate a variety of virtuous and nonvirtuous karma, which are causes of taking rebirth in cyclic existence. In this vein, Dharmakīrti's *Commentary on Valid Cognition* states (2.220d–222a):

Therefore you become attached to your self.
As long as this continues, you will pass through cyclic existence.
Once there is a self, there is a notion of other.
On behalf of self and other, there is attachment and hostility.
All faults come about in association with these.

In this way the ignorance or confusion that apprehends a self, the afflictions of attachment, hostility, and so forth, and the physical, verbal, and mental virtuous and nonvirtuous karmic actions that are motivated by these afflictions are the causes of phenomena—the resources, body, and sites of cyclic existence. Therefore the Buddha taught in the sutras that the causes of cyclic existence are afflictions and karma, that all beings arise from karma, and that mind is the creator of the world. These statements make the same point. And as we saw in the *Dependent Arising Sutra*:

The phenomena that arise from causes,
the Tathāgata proclaimed those causes . . .

In brief, the afflictions of hostility, attachment, and so forth are produced from this life's apprehension of a self, and due to this, you engage in nonvirtuous actions, on account of which you experience suffering. You can understand this process through your own experience. For this process occurs right now, in this lifetime, even in your dreams. In future rebirths as well, whatever thoughts and actions that accord with that lifetime also come from the power of karma and the afflictions.

Regarding the virtuous and nonvirtuous karma that you accumulate throughout your life, there are three possibilities: (1) the karma ripens as a happy or suffering experience in your present life, (2) the karma ripens in your very next life, (3) the karma ripens in some subsequent lifetime. Therefore much of the happiness and suffering of individuals and societies in this world is not just the result of karma planted in previous lives. Principally, in fact, it is the effects of the virtuous or nonvirtuous physical, verbal, and mental karma—the thoughts and deeds—of the present humankind. Consequently, we understand that in this world most of the happiness, suffering, and problems of the societies existing at any particular time are the effects of the physical, verbal, and mental virtuous or nonvirtuous activities of the individuals and societies of that particular time. Then we can understand that whether we will have a happy or miserable society in the future of this world mostly depends on the karma of the thoughts and deeds of the people in the immediately present time.

Question: Can we bring an end to and extinguish this cyclic, everchanging stream of psychophysical aggregates that make up true sufferings?

Answer: The root cause of cyclic existence is the apprehension of a nonexistent, independent self as existing among the aggregates. This apprehension of self is a misapprehension in that it does not accord with reality. Therefore it can be undermined by a mind that knows the nonexistence of an independent self, that accords with reality. By becoming familiar with this mind, you can end this misapprehension.

Suffering is not everlasting. We can bring it to an end along with its cause. Once those who desire liberation eliminate the apprehension of self, the cause of cyclic existence, they will necessarily actualize the truth of cessation of its effect, cyclic existence. So they must cultivate the truth of the path—realization of selflessness—the cause that terminates suffering along with its source. As we saw in the *Dependent Arising Sutra*:

> The phenomena that arise from causes,
> the Tathāgata proclaimed those causes
> as well as their cessation.
> Thus taught the Paragon of Virtue.

Also Dharmakīrti's *Commentary on Valid Cognition* states (2.192bc):

> It is not everlasting
> because it is possible to end its cause and so forth.

Thus liberation from cyclic existence is possible.

Question: The *Rice Seedling Sutra* states:

Monks, whoever sees dependent arising sees the Dharma; whoever sees the Dharma sees the Buddha.

When you see dependent arising, do you necessarily see and know the teachings in detail: the eightfold noble path; the four levels of liberation— stream enterer, once returner, nonreturner, and arhat; the teachings of true cessations; and the teachings of Śākyamuni Buddha?

Answer: In general, when you validly see either the conventional nature (the afflictive dependent arisings) or the ultimate nature (emptiness) you do not necessarily see the pure phenomena (true cessations and the Buddha). Therefore it is not appropriate to take literally a sutra that says, "Whoever sees dependent arising sees the Dharma and the Buddha." The meaning here requires some interpretation.

Question: What is the intended meaning of the sutra that states, "Whoever sees dependent arising sees the Dharma and the Buddha?"

Answer: All afflicted phenomena and pure phenomena are of equal taste in not being ultimately established and lacking true existence. Likewise, when a person who seeks the ontological status of an afflictive phenomenon realizes the reality of afflictive phenomena not being ultimately established, relying on the reasoning of dependent arising and so forth, he or she requires no other reasoning to establish knowledge that other phenomena— such as the Buddha and the teaching of true cessation—are also not ultimately established. They are able to know it in dependence on just that reasoning mentioned above, and thus the sutra makes that statement.

Similarly, when by relying on repeated meditation on emptiness—the true nature of those afflictive phenomena—they finally perceive reality directly, they will also directly perceive the reality of all phenomena, such as the Dharma and the Buddha. With this in mind, the Teacher said in the sutra that whoever sees dependent arising sees the Dharma. In a similar way Nāgārjuna's *Extensive Commentary on the Rice Seedling Sutra* states:

Both the statement from the sutra that says "whoever sees this dependent arising" and [the line in my verse] that says "that which lacks life [self] and so on" mean that whoever sees this dependent arising always sees the lack of life and so on. That is to say, they see the lack of life, they are aware of it, they engage it inferentially, they understand it, they realize it, and they thoroughly know it.[136]

Āryadeva's *Four Hundred Stanzas* says (8.191):

> Whoever sees the emptiness of one thing
> is said to see the emptiness of all things.
> The emptiness of one thing is
> the emptiness of all things.

Haribhadra's *Clarification of the Meaning Commentary* states:

> One thing has the nature of all things.
> All things have the nature of all things.
> Whoever sees the reality of one thing
> sees the reality of all things.[137]

The *King of Concentration Sutra* states:

> When you understand the real nature,
> there is nothing at all to be said about it.
> By the one, you also understand all.
> By the one, you also see all.[138]

Therefore the dependent arisings of the afflicted class, the teachings of truth of the path and truth of cessation of the pure class, and the teachings of the Buddha are of the same taste in being ultimately empty of inherent establishment. Likewise, when you directly see the emptiness that is the perfectly established character of any dependently arisen phenomenon, you are abiding in a noble being's sublime wisdom of equality that does not observe phenomena as being different. It is also equal in directly seeing emptiness, the perfectly established character of the Dharma and the Buddha. Considering such equality, the Buddha stated in the sutra that whoever sees dependent arising sees the Dharma and the Buddha.

From among the four types of sutras whose meaning can be interpreted based on context, this sutra is said to be one whose context intends a meaning of equality. Also among the four types of sutras with circuitous intention, it is a sutra that intends a circuitous meaning regarding the character of phenomena.[139] Kamalaśīla's *Detailed Commentary on the Rice Seedling Sutra* states:

> Whoever understands dependent arising that was spoken thus will know the teachings of noble beings. This has the meaning of "understanding ultimate phenomena."[140]

And also:

> Consequently, when you know the teachings of noble beings, you have genuine sublime wisdom. Therefore, when this yogi sees the dependent arising that was spoken thus, he or she "sees the Dharma and the Buddha." The Blessed One stated this. Therefore the Buddha taught with the contextual intention of equality and the circuitous intention of perfectly established character. The Blessed One intended that there be no contradiction with regard to his words.[141]

7. The Factors of Dependent Arising

THE FORWARD AND REVERSE ORDER
OF DEPENDENT ARISING

In the *Rice Seedling Sutra*, Maitreya describes the process of dependent arising in terms of the twelve factors, beginning with ignorance and culminat-
ing in birth and in aging and death (which he expands to encompass
"sorrow, lamentation, misery, unhappiness, and conflict"). The *Rice Seedling Sutra* begins by listing them in their forward order:

> That is, dependent on ignorance, conditioning factors occur;
> dependent on conditioning factors, consciousness; dependent
> on consciousness, name-and-form; dependent on name-and-
> form, the six sense-bases; dependent on the six sense-bases,
> contact; dependent on contact, feeling; dependent on feeling,
> craving; dependent on craving, grasping; dependent on grasp-
> ing, becoming; dependent on becoming, birth; dependent on
> birth occur aging and death, sorrow, lamentation, misery, unhap-
> piness, and conflict. This entire great heap of suffering occurs in
> that way.

Question: When the *Rice Seedling Sutra* states: "Dependent on ignorance, conditioning factors occur," this explicitly indicates the forward
order of afflicted factors of dependent arising that follow ignorance and
implicitly indicates the reverse order. The statement "with the ceasing of
ignorance, conditioning factors cease" explicitly indicates the forward
order of pure factors of dependent arising and implicitly indicates the
reverse order. How do these two systems work?

Answer: Kamalaśila's *Detailed Commentary on the Rice Seedling Sutra* states: "In order to free from confusion those who are bewildered about entering and reversing cyclic existence, dependent arising is taught, covering the afflicted class of phenomena and the pure class of phenomena in both the forward and the reverse orders."[142]

The forward and reverse orders of both classes of phenomena are indicated in order to clear away confusion and hone a skillful understanding of the four noble truths: how one enters cyclic existence, where true sufferings are the effect and true origins are the cause; and the freedom of reversing cyclic existence, where true cessations are the effect and true paths are the cause. That is, you divide both afflicted phenomena and pure phenomena into forward and reverse orders. As the noble Asaṅga's *Compendium of the Mahayana* states: "How is there both a forward order and a reverse order? The forward and reverse orders of dependent arising are taught by way of the forward and reverse orders of afflicted phenomena and the forward and reverse orders of pure phenomena."[143]

Question: With respect to how to meditate on dependent arising, there are meditations on both conventional dependent arising and ultimate dependent arising. How do you meditate on the forward order and reverse order of conventional dependent arising?

Answer: You meditate according to the order of the four noble truths. The noble Asaṅga's *Compendium of Determinations* states:

Consequently, you analyze true sufferings and true origins of suffering in accordance with the reverse order of dependent arising and the forward order of dependent arising, respectively. Thereafter, you want to analyze true cessations and then use the reverse order from aging and death to ignorance. What is the reason for this? If you ask, "How would I have permanently ended these current true sufferings, those that have already arisen," you think, "These would have ceased when I no longer created new karma that arises from the condition of ignorance." After you have thus analyzed these three noble truths, you start searching and think, "What is the path to attain this true cessation? What is the measure of this path?" By remembering the conditions in a former life, you clearly know and think over how you previously taught the personal instructions for eradicating faults, the correct worldly view. Then you think, "I previously reached the path repeatedly traveled by the earlier sages." This is the investigation of the four truths, just the contemplation of conventional dependent arising.[144]

This is how you meditate on the reverse order of the afflicted factors of dependent arising: You contemplate again and again the principal sufferings that are self-evident—aging, death, sorrow, lamentation, misery, unhappiness, conflict, and so forth. Then, when you investigate where these sufferings of aging and death and so forth arise from, you reflect that they arise from the condition of taking birth into cyclic existence and assuming the contaminated aggregates. When you then investigate the origin of this birth in cyclic existence, you reflect on how it arose from the condition of becoming, which is karma. In this way, you contemplate step by step the remaining factors of dependent arising, the way the latter ones arise based on the former ones. Finally, when you investigate the origin of the second factor of dependent arising—conditioning factors, or compositional activity—you see that it arises due to ignorance. From repeatedly meditating up to this point, you understand the nature of true sufferings, cyclic existence, and then, by producing aversion to it, you generate the desire to be free from it and become expert regarding true sufferings.

The subsequent meditation on the forward order of the afflicted factors of dependent arising is as follows: you think about how conditioning factors arise due to ignorance, the grasping at self that, from the outset, apprehends a self and that which belongs to a self. Likewise, you contemplate the arising of consciousness due to conditioning factors and so forth, how the latter factors of dependent arising arise from the former ones. Finally, you repeatedly contemplate and meditate on how sufferings such as aging, death, sorrow, lamentation, and so forth arise because of birth. From this you gain clear knowledge of cyclic existence—your successive rebirths in this cyclic existence due to karma and the afflictions—and become expert regarding true origins, producing a desire to eliminate suffering and its causes.

The meditation on the reverse order of pure dependent arising is as follows: after fully contemplating the way of suffering of cyclic existence—

aging, death, sorrow, lamentation, misery, unhappiness, conflict, and so on—you think, "By ceasing what cause can I end these sufferings?" Then you contemplate and meditate repeatedly on the factors of dependent arising, thinking in succession that by ceasing birth in cyclic existence you cease aging and death, by ceasing the karma that is becoming you end birth in cyclic existence and so on, until finally thinking that by ceasing ignorance you end conditioning factors. From this you see that you are able to eliminate these sufferings of cyclic existence—aging, death, and so forth—and obtain a true cessation. Thereafter, you become expert regarding the cessation that eliminates suffering. Once you have generated the desire to obtain that cessation, in order to do so you study, reflect, and meditate on the non-existence of an independent, ultimately existent self—the referent object that is exactly what ignorance, the root of cyclic existence, apprehends as its object. Thereby you understand that you must meditate on true paths and enter into the practice of true paths.

The meditation on the forward order of pure dependent arising is as follows: from directly perceiving the lack of an independent self, you are unable to motivate karma impelled by the apprehension of a self. Thereupon, you end fundamental ignorance, thereby ending conditioning factors, and you meditate, applying this process to the remaining factors of dependent arising. Finally, you reflect repeatedly on and meditate on the way in which the ceasing of birth ceases aging, death, sorrow, lamentation, and so forth. From this you become expert in the truth of the path, which is the cause of cutting the root of suffering, the apprehension of a self. With enthusiasm you engage in meditating on the path of selflessness.

Therefore, from meditation on the reverse orders of the afflicted and the pure phenomena, you are freed from obscuration regarding true sufferings and true cessations, respectively. From the meditations on the forward order you are freed from obscuration regarding true origins and true paths. Thus the protector Nāgārjuna stated in his *Fundamental Verses on the Middle Way* (24.40):

One who sees dependent arising
sees true sufferings,
true origins, true cessations,
and true paths.

Also, Je Tsongkhapa stated in his *Questions with Virtuous High Resolve*:

> Furthermore, if we do not have a vivid experience of how we pass in succession from one type of life to the next in this cyclic existence, we will not have an actual revulsion for cyclic existence, an actual disenchantment with it, or an actual determination to be free of it. Production of such a vivid experience of how we wander in cyclic existence depends on meditation on how a person cycles by means of the twelve factors of dependent arising.[145]

And he states in his stages of the path poem *Songs of Experience*:

> If you do not strive to contemplate the faults of true sufferings,
> you will not be squarely intent on liberation.
> If you do not think about true origins, the stages of entering cyclic existence,
> you will not know how to sever the root of cyclic existence.
> Thus treasure reliance on disenchantment, the determination to be free of cyclic existence,
> as well as the knowledge of what binds you to cyclic existence.[146]

Question: The *Rice Seedling Sutra* states: "By ceasing ignorance, you cease conditioning factors," and so on. If this describes the forward order of pure factors of dependent arising, doesn't it contradict Kamalaśīla's *Detailed Commentary* where it states, "In order to free from confusion those who are bewildered about entering and exiting from cyclic existence, dependent arising is taught, covering the afflicted class of phenomena and the pure class of phenomena by both the forward order and reverse order"?[147] He explains the teaching of the forward order by saying, "Due to ignorance, conditioning factors arise" and the "non-forward," or reverse order, by saying, "By ceasing ignorance, conditioning factors cease."

Answer: The first sutra citation just stated shows the order of conditioning factors after ignorance by showing that conditioning factors arise due to the condition of ignorance. The second sutra citation is showing the cessation of conditioning factors by ceasing ignorance. Both of these together show the cause-and-effect relationship between the successive factors of dependent arising in both the forward and reverse ways. Kamalaśīla's *Detailed Commentary on the Rice Seedling Sutra* states:

> When the sutra says, "Here, due to the condition of ignorance, conditioning factors arise," this statement shows that there is certainly no doubt that the capacity of ignorance and so on is that they are cause-and-effect phenomena. This is dependent arising.[148]

Therefore the sutra statement "By ceasing ignorance, you cease conditioning factors" and so on shows the stages of the reverse relationship [between cause and effect] wherein you end conditioning factors and so forth by ending ignorance. This does not contradict showing the forward order of the pure factors of dependent arising; both have a similar meaning.

Analyzing the Cessation of Ignorance and So On

Question: What is the meaning of *ceasing* in the statement, "By ceasing ignorance you cease conditioning factors"?

Answer: When, for instance, a seed ceases the moment a sprout is produced, this is not the sense of cessation intended here. Were the cessation of ignorance like this, then when ignorance ceased, the effect of conditioning factors would still be produced; there would be no cessation of conditioning factors. Therefore *ceasing* in this statement is not to be taken as cessation in the sense of a cause ceasing the moment the effect is produced.

Furthermore, arhats simultaneously abandon ignorance, craving, and grasping. They also must simultaneously abandon the other factors of dependent arising and later cast aside the factors that start from the third factor of dependent arising (consciousness) up to the seventh factor (feeling) as well as birth and aging and death. Therefore it is inappropriate to take "ignorance ceases" to mean that ignorance is "cast aside" or "abandoned."

Composite phenomena perish automatically. Their destruction is not necessarily contingent on some other cause or condition arising from it. Therefore it is unsuitable to take the statement, "By ceasing ignorance, you cease conditioning factors" to mean ordinary perishing.

Nevertheless, Vasubandhu's *Explaining the First Factor of Dependent Arising and Its Divisions* states:

> If *cessation* means "eradication" it would be unsuitable to teach cessation in stages. You eradicate ignorance, craving, and grasping simultaneously, and once you eradicate those factors, you posit the eradication of the other factors.[149]

And also:

> If the cessation of ignorance and so forth were understood to be their destruction, this would invalidate momentary destruction. You would have to assert that from the cause being destroyed the effect would be destroyed.[150]

Therefore the meaning of "ceasing ignorance" and so forth is as follows: After determining through study and reflection the selflessness that is the lack of a substantially established person, you meditate on it again and again.[151] From this, you produce in your mind the noble path that is the direct knowledge of selflessness, which does not accord with the ignorance that apprehends a self, which motivates the karma that propels rebirth in cyclic existence. Thereupon, you stop newly accumulating the karma that, motivated by the apprehension of a self, propels rebirth in cyclic existence. Therefore, by the cessation and nonproduction of initial ignorance, the second factor of conditioning factors is not produced and is thus said to "cease."

The master Kamalaśīla's *Detailed Commentary on the Rice Seedling Sutra* states:

> *Question*: How can you say that the cessation of ignorance and so on is also a dependent arising [i.e., an existent]?
>
> *Answer*: There is no fault here. In this case, the phrase "ceasing of ignorance and so on" is not stated in reference to a nonaffirming negative. Like eating an essential-energy pill,[152] by the power of having become accustomed to the path [of selflessness], you produce an awareness that does not accord with ignorance. Thus it is said that ignorance ceases, because in this awareness or

through this awareness you end the ignorance that is a misconception and so on.[153]

Therefore, as Kamalaśīla states, the production of an awareness that is not in accord with ignorance is the cessation intended here, a gradual cessation of ignorance, followed by the cessation of conditioning factors and the remaining factors of dependent arising, one by one.

How to Divide the Twelve Factors of Dependent Arising into Three Lifetimes

Question: The *Rice Seedling Sutra* states: "Dependent on ignorance, conditioning factors occur," and so on. Does this indicate that the descriptions of the twelve factors of dependent arising—from ignorance up to aging and death—are one sequence of dependent arising for a single lifetime? Or do they span multiple lifetimes?

Answer: The twelve factors of dependent arising, in order, are not taught from the perspective of one lifetime. Why? Say it were one lifetime. Craving and grasping nurture the karma that impels birth and then you are born. After birth, feelings arise once name-and-form, the six sense-bases, and contact are established. Clearly, you would have to accept that the eighth factor, craving, gives rise to the seventh factor, feeling. You couldn't say, "Due to the condition of feeling, craving arises." This is the reason that the explanation where craving arises conditioned by feeling has to describe the production of craving in one sequence of dependent arising as coming from feeling in another sequence of dependent arising. Je Tsongkhapa's *Great Treatise* states:

> Therefore the two factors of craving, which is an actualizing factor, and feeling, which gives rise to this craving, are not in the same sequence of dependent arising. The feeling that gives rise to craving is an effect of some other sequence of dependent arising.[154]

Thus the feeling that generates craving, the eighth factor, is a result that has ripened in the present lifetime. The craving that is then produced from that feeling in turn serves as a causal factor of dependent arising that will give rise to the next life after the present one, a life that will include the factor of feeling. Therefore both the seventh factor, feeling, and the eighth factor, craving, of a single sequence of twelve factors stem from different sequences of dependent arising comprising separate lifetimes.

Question: These twelve factors of dependent arising are posited from the viewpoint of two different sequences of dependent arising in both a former and future lifetime. How are they then posited in three parts for three lifetimes?

Answer: The master Kamalaśīla's *Detailed Commentary on the Rice Seedling Sutra* states: "The first three are projecting factors."[155] He is indicating that the first factor of ignorance, the second factor of conditioning factors, and the third factor of consciousness are *projecting* factors. Take the example of Dharmadatta's present lifetime. Those three projecting factors exist in some other lifetime prior to Dharmadatta's present life. The fourth through seventh factors—name-and-form, the six sense-bases, contact, and feeling— are *projected* factors. They exist in Dharmadatta's present lifetime. These projecting factors are causes and the projected factors are their effects. These are factors of dependent arising of the same sequence. Both the eighth factor, craving, and the ninth factor, grasping, which nurture the karma that projects Dharmadatta's future lifetime, as well as the tenth factor, becoming, which is the karmic potency that has been made active by those two factors, are the *actualizing* factors. These three are also in Dharmadatta's present lifetime. After Dharmadatta transitions from this life, he is reborn into his future life, where both the eleventh factor, birth, and the twelfth factor, aging and death, are *actualized factors*. These two occur in the lifetime that immediately follows Dharmadatta's present life. These actualizing causes and actualized effects are in the same sequence of dependent arising.[156]

Question: Summarizing the causes of the present life, the Buddha described only three factors of dependent arising in a former lifetime— ignorance, conditioning factors, and the causal consciousness that carries a karmic potency. Summarizing the effects in the next lifetime, he described as actualized effects only birth and aging and death. Therefore the factors of dependent arising related to the effect that is the present lifetime are only seven—the projecting factors of ignorance, conditioning factors, and consciousness and the four projected effects of name-and-form up to feeling. Thus the twelve factors related to the present lifetime are incomplete. Likewise, for the sequence that produces the next lifetime, there are only five factors—the three actualizing causal factors of craving, grasping, and becoming and the two actualized effects of birth and aging and death. Why are the twelve factors not all present for each lifetime?

Answer: There is no fault. The Buddha summarized a previous lifetime's causes of this present life, directly indicating just three factors—ignorance, conditioning factors, and consciousness. And he described only the three factors of craving, grasping, and becoming as factors in this middle lifetime that are the causes of the next lifetime. What can you infer from these? The causes existing in a previous lifetime must include not only the projecting causes of ignorance, conditioning factors, and consciousness, but also, by inference that draws from the description of this middle lifetime, the actualizing causes of craving, grasping, and becoming as well. Likewise, as effects described in the next lifetime, the Buddha mentioned just the actualized effects of birth and aging and death. However, you can also infer from the example of this middle lifetime that name-and-form, sense-bases, contact, and feeling also exist in the next life when there is birth and aging and death. Similarly, the master Vasubandhu states in his *Treasury of Knowledge* (3.25):

> Inferring from the middle lifetime,
> the causes and effects of the two lifetimes are summarized.

Therefore whatever is an effect projected by the projecting causes must be an effect actualized by the actualizing causes. Likewise, whatever is an effect actualized by the actualizing causes must be an effect projected by the three projecting causes.[157]

Nevertheless, it is possible that there also exists in between the projecting causes and projected effects of, for instance, a human rebirth, many lifetimes of other dependent-arising sequences of an animal and so forth. The actualizing causes—craving, grasping, and becoming—must actualize the effect that is projected by the projecting causes. As ignorance, conditioning factors, and consciousness act as distant causes of some lifetime, they are called *projecting causes*. As it is not possible for the lifetime of another dependent-arising sequence to exist in between the actualizing causes—craving, grasping, and becoming—and their actualized effect, they act as nearby causes of any lifetime and are thus called *actualizing causes*.

Question: When the Buddha taught the twelve factors of dependent arising in the sutras, he did not describe the order of the twelve factors of one sequence from the viewpoint of a single lifetime. He summarized a portion of the causes in a former lifetime and briefly indicated a portion of the effects in the next lifetime. He described in more detail the projected effects and actualizing causes in this middle lifetime. Why did he do it this way?

Answer: There is great purpose. As explained above, by this description you are able to understand the existence of the twelve factors in both previous and future lifetimes. From the effect factors that were produced in a prior lifetime arise the causal factors for the next lifetime. This continues from one lifetime to the next. It is a teaching that illustrates the way of cycling.

Echoing the above explanation from Kamalaśīla's *Detailed Commentary on the Rice Seedling Sutra*, Asaṅga's *Compendium of Knowledge* also states, "What are the projecting factors? They are ignorance, conditioning factors, and consciousness."[158] It also states, "Any conditioning factors, consciousness, and becoming are included in afflicted karma." Although the consciousness in the causal period of carrying the predisposing latencies of karma is not karma itself, it is a basis that possesses the karmic potency. It is therefore folded in with karma and described as a cause that projects a lifetime. Thus there are six causal factors and six effect factors.

Question: Vasubandhu's *Treasury of Knowledge* states (3.20):

Consciousness is the connecting aggregate [at conception].

And also (3.24):

Both the former lifetime and the next lifetime each have two [factors of dependent arising].

This first statement describes the consciousness factor of dependent arising as the effect consciousness at the time of conception in the next lifetime. The second statement indicates only two factors of dependent arising—ignorance and conditioning factors—as factors that occur in a former lifetime. That makes five causal factors and seven effect factors. Aren't this and the former explanation of the twelve factors of dependent arising contradictory?

Answer: The *Treasury of Knowledge*'s description, which expresses the Vaibhāṣika's position, asserts, "occasion dependent arising."[159] The prior explanation above is the system of the upper Abhidharma school and the Madhyamaka school. So there is no contradiction.

DO THE TWELVE FACTORS EXIST
IN ALL THREE REALMS?

This question also has different interpretations. The master Pūrṇavardhana in *Following the Definitions*, his commentary on the *Treasury of Knowledge*, says:

> I will comment on [the *Treasury* verse lines 3.21d–22a] "Name-and-form exists from [consciousness] up to the formation of the six sense-bases." Thus there are not twelve factors in the form realm [due to spontaneous birth]. For one who enters the form-less realm, there is no occasion for either name-and-form or the six sense-bases. As form does not exist there, neither do these two factors, leaving only ten factors.[160]

Wherever the spontaneously born beings of the form realm take rebirth, their sensory faculties are complete, simultaneous with their conception, so at no time are there no six sense-bases. Therefore the dependent arising factor of name-and-form does not exist in the form realm. For one who is reborn in the formless realm there is no form at all. As there is neither name-and-form nor the five sense-bases that have form for the fifth factor of sense-bases, Pūrṇavardhana states that there are ten factors in the formless realm.

Asaṅga explains this differently in his *Yogic Levels*:

> How do the twelve factors of dependent arise in the desire realm? They are all present there and in complete form. How are they present in the form realm? They are all there but only par-tial. What is the nature of aging there? The form aggregate is old and faded. Just as they are in the form realm, so they are in the formless realm.[161]

Asaṅga says that in the desire realm the twelve factors are complete in all aspects whereas in the form realm they are complete merely in their enumeration, since some are incomplete. Furthermore, in the formless realm the fourth factor, name-and-form, has no form but does have the dependent arising of name. Also, the fifth factor, six sense-bases, does not have the five sense-bases that have form but is partial in the sense of having the sixth sense-base, the mental sense-base. Therefore, Asaṅga can say that there are twelve factors even for one born in the formless realm.

The above statement by the master Pūrṇavardhana is the Vaibhāṣika system. The latter statements from noble Asaṅga's *Yogic Levels* are necessarily commentary in the system of upper Abhidharma. These two different ways are distinct systems, so they are not contradictory. Again, Vasubandhu's *Treasury of Knowledge* (3.21–22) states:

> Consciousness is the connecting aggregate [at conception].
> Name-and-form exists from [consciousness]
> up to the formation of the six sense-bases.

According to the Vaibhāṣika system, the factor of name-and-form lasts from the first moment of the effect consciousness, which begins with conception, also known as the birth stage, up to the formation of the six sense-bases. In upper Abhidharma, conception and the establishment of the fourth factor, name-and-form, are simultaneous. The *Treasury of Knowledge* itself also asserts that those two are simultaneous.

Moreover, the noble Asaṅga states in his *Yogic Levels*,

> *Question*: Why are name-and-form and consciousness presented as conditions for one another?
> *Answer*: Name-and-form is the condition for consciousness in this lifetime, and consciousness is the condition for the name-and-form of the next lifetime. When conception occurs in the mother's womb, they are each the condition for the other. Due to the condition of consciousness, the form that is the semen and ovum in the mother's womb is imbued with the aggregate of name [i.e. consciousness], which abides together with form in the initial state of embryonic transformation.[162] The consciousness that arises from the condition of name-and-form thereby finds its place.[163]

Also, Vasubandhu's *Treasury of Knowledge Autocommentary* states:

> Preceded by consciousness, name-and-form consists of the five aggregates that are reborn as this or that being. This is taught in the *Exegesis of the Discipline*.[164]

The third factor, consciousness, is said to last up until life in the intermediate state has finished. When the form aggregate is created, due to the condition of this consciousness, it is asserted that a being enters the birth
stage—in other words, it is reborn. In agreement with this the *Rice Seedling
Sutra* states:

> Consciousness arising together with the four formless aggregates
> and the form [aggregate] are called "dependent on conscious-
> ness, name-and-form."

At this point in the sutra, Kamalaśīla's commentary on it similarly states:

> Because of which, the ripening of name-and-form is actualized
> simultaneously with the consciousness that is a ripening.[165]

He is saying that the fourth factor of dependent arising, name-and-form,
exists simultaneously with the consciousness that is the ripening of former
karma and that comprises the birth stage.[166]

Nāgārjuna also similarly states in his *Extensive Commentary on the Rice
Seedling Sutra*:

> "Also with that is the afflicted mind"[167] means that the afflicted
> mind and the four elements assemble together, and this is known
> as *name-and-form*, which are related in the manner of a support
> beam and a house. With respect to this, *name* refers to the four
> non-form aggregates of feeling, discrimination, compositional
> factors, and consciousness. *Form* refers to what arises from the
> parents' sperm and ovum. Name-and-form is that which is first
> actualized in dependence on the aggregate of the intermediate
> state being. [The parents' regenerative fluids], together with the
> afflicted mind—the contaminated mental consciousness that
> has a nature that is obscured, ethically neutral, and possesses four
> afflictions: ignorance regarding self, pride regarding self, view of
> the self, and attachment to self—is called *name-and-form*.[168]

8. How the Self Exists

The Self That Does Not Exist

Question: Vasubandhu's *Treasury of Knowledge* (3.18) states:

> There is no self, just the aggregates.

The *Rice Seedling Sutra* and its commentaries explain that there is no self that is an entity separate from the aggregates, a self coming from the former life to this life, a self transmigrating from this life to another life and so forth. Do Buddhists assert that there is no self or person who is the one who experiences happiness and suffering?

Answer: No proponent of Buddhist tenets whatsoever asserts a self that is an entity separate from the aggregates or a self that is permanent, unitary, and independent. The Prasaṅgika Mādhyamikas do not even assert a self that is established by way of its own entity. Why is that? If the self were permanent, unitary, and independent like the non-Buddhists assert, then the self that appropriates the aggregates of the former life, this life, and the future life would be the same self without any difference, while the aggregates that are appropriated would be separate from that self. This is incorrect. If the self and the aggregates had distinct essences, that would be correct, but the self and the aggregates are not like that. For if the self had a discrete essence different from the aggregates, then, like distinguishing blue from yellow, you would be able to identify a self that does not depend on the appropriated aggregates, but you cannot. If the self and the aggregates existed as independent and separate entities, they would have no connection to each other and would not be mutually dependent. Like a pot and a woolen cloth, it would be necessary to observe them as different individual items. Therefore, like a flower in the sky, a self that is an entity separate from the aggregates does not exist. Nāgārjuna's *Fundamental Verses on the Middle Way* (27.17) states:

> A self that is different
> from the appropriated [aggregates] is not possible.
> If it were different, then it would be observed
> without appropriation. But it is not observed.

Furthermore, it is not logical to assert, as do the Buddhist essentialists, a self that is separate from the appropriated aggregates. Any self presumed to exist from its own side among the aggregates would in fact be merely a synonym for the aggregates. Thus to say, as an essentialist would, that there is an inherently existent self would be senseless.

If the aggregates *were* the self itself, or the self and the aggregates were essentially existent and of one intrinsic nature, then it would follow that in whatever way the aggregates were produced and perished—whether the appropriated aggregates were destroyed or a new continuum of the aggregates arose and so on—the production and perishing of the self would have to be just the same. Moreover, there would be many faults, such as the consequence that the aggregates that are appropriated and the self that is the appropriator would be the same. Nāgārjuna's *Fundamental Verses on the Middle Way* (27.8) states:

> Thus [the self] is neither different from the appropriator
> nor identical to the appropriator.

And also (18.1):

> If the self were the aggregates,
> it would have to arise and cease.
> If it were different from the aggregates,
> it would not share the characteristics of the aggregates.

The Self That Does Exist

Question: The appropriated aggregates are not the self, and the self is not some other entity or substance distinct from the aggregates. Does this mean then the self does not exist?

Answer: It makes no sense to say the appropriated aggregates exist but the self that is the appropriator does not. As the self is imputed in dependence on the appropriated aggregates, if the self were completely nonexistent, it would make no sense to impute a self in dependence on the aggregates, like you can't impute the nonexistent son of a barren woman in dependence on the aggregates. The *Clear Words* of the master Candrakīrti states:

> The self is not of the same nature as the appropriated because this would entail that the appropriated and the appropriator would be the same and also that the self would arise and perish [like the aggregates]. The self is not separate from the appropriated aggregates because this would mean the self could be identified separately, without depending on the appropriated aggregates. Also, the self is not apprehended without apprehending the appropriated because this would entail identifying a self that does not depend on the appropriated aggregates.
>
> You might think, "If that is so, then don't you have to say that the self does not exist?" However, it is also *not* the case that the self does not exist. For how can you say that that which is imputed in dependence on the aggregates does not exist? How can you say that, like the son of a barren woman—something completely nonexistent—it is not imputed in dependence on the aggregates? How could it be possible to say that the appropriator does not exist while the appropriated does exist? Thus the nonexistence of the self is also not tenable, and it is not correct to say that the self does not exist.
>
> The description of this self can be ascertained in detail in my *Entering the Middle Way* [6.120–65]. Because I have already described it at several points here in this work, I will not present it again here.[169]

Therefore the self is not completely the same as the aggregates, nor is the self a totally different entity or substance from the aggregates. However, we can posit a self that is a mere imputation in dependence on the aggregates. It is then feasible that there is a self that: (1) changes and is one nature with the aggregates,[170] (2) has parts, and (3) is other-powered in being dependent on the aggregates.

Question: How is the self presented in Candrakīrti's *Entering the Middle Way*, as *Clear Words* mentions?

Answer: The way that Candrakīrti presents the self in his *Entering the Middle Way* is as follows. He begins by quoting a sutra:

> "Self" is a demonic mind.
> You have a wrong view.
> These composite aggregates are empty;
> there is no living being in them.
>
> Just as one speaks of a chariot
> in dependence upon collections of parts,
> so we use the convention "living being"
> in dependence upon the aggregates.[171]

According to this sutra, as there is no self in the aggregates that exists substantially in the sense of being independent, it is unsuitable to believe such a self exists. If you take the example of a chariot, neither each part of the chariot nor the collection of parts is the chariot, and there is also no chariot that is some substance separate from those. Nonetheless, in dependence on the collection of chariot parts, we posit chariot as a mere imputation, saying "this chariot." Likewise, while none of the aggregates are the self and there is no self that is a substance or entity separate from these aggregates, the sutra states that we must posit a self by mere imputation in dependence on the aggregates. Candrakīrti's *Entering the Middle Way* (6.132) states:

> Now you may claim that the Teacher said the aggregates
>   are the self,
> so you assert the aggregates to be the self.
> But the Buddha's statement refutes a self separate from
>   the aggregates;
> in other sutras he explained that form is not the self.

And also (6.135ab):

> Were it not so, if we compare the chariot to the self,
> the mere collection of a chariot's parts would constitute a chariot.

Well then, if there were a self that is permanent, unitary, and independent, the selves of three lifetimes—former, present, and future—would be the same. If this were so, the present life's self would exist in both the former and future lifetimes. In addition, the independently existing self within the present body would migrate by entering into the body of the future lifetime. Accordingly, when someone is born as a human after a lifetime as a god, if the two selves of a god and a human existed from their own sides, that person would have to be both a god and a human that were independent and distinct, like yellow and blue. If they were like this, they could not both be part of the same continuum. If they were the same and independent, such a human would be both a human and a god. Nāgārjuna's *Fundamental Verses on the Middle Way* (27.15) states:

> If a human were a god,
> in such a view there would be permanence.

And also (27.16):

> If the human were different from the god,
> a continuum would not be possible.

There Is No Self That Blends Different Time Periods

Many wrong views arise from imagining either a permanent self or a self established from its own side. For instance, some people assume that the present, independent self existed in the previous life. Others think, similarly, that this present self will be reborn into a future life. Some, like the Cārvākas, believe there is no future life, that the continuum ceases at the time of death.

Whether the self is permanent, inherently established, or conventionally existent, it is said that the self of the former time does not transfer to a future time. The *Rice Seedling Sutra* states:

> External dependent arisings are to be seen as fivefold. What five?
> Not eternalism, not annihilation, not transmigration, a great
> result arises from a small cause, and the continuity of what is
> similar to that.

Kamalaśīla's *Detailed Commentary on the Rice Seedling Sutra* states:

As cause and effect are not the same, there is no transference.[172]

In the context of explaining internal dependent arising having five characteristics, the *Rice Seedling Sutra* states:

How is [internal dependent arising] not transmigration? From different species of beings [e.g., humans and gods] arises birth in a common species, and therefore [internal dependent arising] is not transmigration.

On this point, Kamalaśīla's *Detailed Commentary on the Rice Seedling Sutra* states:

"Different" here means to be reborn from one class of beings, such as humans, into another class of beings, such as gods.[173]

Consequently, a fixed self separate from the aggregates does not exist, so it cannot be the same self across the past, present, and future lifetimes. This present self that is particular to this lifetime does not transfer to the next lifetime. Nonetheless, the *Rice Seedling Sutra* states:

Regarding that, while indeed no dharma at all passes from this world to the next, because causes and conditions are not deficient, the result of karma appears. Thus, for example, though the reflection of a face appears in the orb of a clean mirror while indeed the face is not transferred to the mirror, because the causes and conditions are not deficient, a face appears. Likewise, no one departs from this world and is born in another, but because the causes and conditions are not deficient, the result of karma appears.

Thus, for example, the orb of the moon wanders 42,000 yojanas above; nevertheless, the reflection of the orb of the moon appears in a small vessel filled with water even though the orb of the moon is not transferred from that place. While indeed the moon does not go inside the small water-filled vessel, because the causes and conditions are not deficient, the orb of the moon appears. Likewise, while indeed no one departs from this world and is born in another, because causes and conditions are not deficient, the result of karma appears.

Thus, for example, fire does not flame when causes and conditions are deficient, but from causes and conditions gathering, fire flames. Similarly, because causes and conditions are not deficient in those dharmas without a governor, without [the notion] "mine," without grasping, equal to space, and having the essential nature of the mark of illusion, a consciousness that is a seed germinated by karma and defilement produces the sprout of name-and-form in this or that mother's womb, the place of birth, reconnection. In that way, the dependence on conditions of internal dependent arising is to be seen.

How the Self of This Lifetime Transitions into the Next

Because an oil lamp's flame is momentary, the previous moment's flame does not transfer into the next moment; a mere continuum of moments of the lamp's flame goes into the next moment without interruption. Likewise, although the consciousness and the self of Dharmadatta in this lifetime do not transfer to the next lifetime unchanged, due to the aggregation of afflictions and karma a mere continuum of the aggregates of consciousness and the four other aggregates is conceived in the womb of the mother, the birthplace of the next lifetime. There is no contradiction in this.

Many examples are taught regarding this: (1) When masters teach their disciples a daily prayer recitation by having them repeat the lines of prayer after them, the daily recitation is not transferred to the disciples, but the disciples know the recitation just as the masters do. (2) Although a face is not transferred into a mirror, a reflection arises. Similarly, (3) an impression arises from a seal, (4) fire arises from a magnifying glass, (5) your mouth secretes saliva when you see something sour or hear someone talk about something sour or see someone experiencing something sour, (6) a sprout arises from a seed, and (7) an echo arises from a sound. In all these cases, something does not transfer to another place, but from the completion of the dependent arising of causes and conditions, they arise in that way. The

Buddha taught the arising of a being's future life through these examples. In the same vein, Nāgārjuna's *Essence of Dependent Arising* states:

> Recitation, oil lamp, mirror, seal,
> magnifying glass, seed, something sour, and a sound.
> With these, the learned know that the conception
>   of the aggregates
> also takes place without being transferred.[174]

Vasubandhu's *Presentation of Reason* states:

> The Blessed One says in the *Sutra of Ultimate Emptiness*, "Karma exists. Maturation also exists. However, do not observe an agent."
>
> *Question*: Is this statement speaking ultimately or conventionally?
>
> *Answer*: What are you asking? If it were ultimately, how would all phenomena be devoid of essence? If the Buddha were speaking conventionally, the Buddha would not say that the agent does not exist. The agent would also exist conventionally.
>
> *Question*: First, what is this "conventional?" What is "the ultimate?" What should we understand to exist conventionally and what to exist ultimately?
>
> *Answer*: We say that name, expression, imputation, and convention are conventional. The self-characteristic of phenomena is the ultimate.
>
> *Question*: Well then, karma and maturation both exist in name and by their self-characteristic.
>
> *Answer*: Therefore it is appropriate to understand them in whatever way you want. I say that the person exists conventionally but not substantially, because its name is imputed to the aggregates.[175]

This is saying that, although there is karma and maturation, there is no self of this lifetime that is an agent that is transferred to the next lifetime. This passage also indicates a difference between Buddhist and non-Buddhist assertions. Udbhatasiddhasvamin's *Praise of the Exalted One* states:

[Others] accept that a subtle life force [i.e., a self] transfers
from this body into another body.
You [the Buddha] said, "A life force that is separate from the body
does not exist."[176]

Nāgārjuna's *Verses on the Rice Seedling Sutra* states:

Nothing whatsoever goes
from this world to the beyond.
Nevertheless, from causes and conditions,
the effect of karma manifests.
This is just as, in a clean mirror,
one sees the image of a face
but the image does not
transfer into the mirror,
and just as the distant moon
appears in a small vessel of water
but is not transferred there.
Karma and its functions exist.
Likewise, at death nothing transfers
from this life, but a being is born.
If the causes and conditions are not complete,
   a fire does not burn.
Once they are complete, the fire burns.
So, from complete causes and conditions,
the aggregates of a new life arise.
Just like the moon reflected in water,
nothing transfers from here at death,
but a being is reborn.[177]

Nāgārjuna's autocommentary to these verses states:

Since nothing whatsoever transfers from this world to the next
or from the previous one to this one, don't you have to propose
permanence, no cause, or a discordant cause? The Buddha said,
because the causes and conditions are complete, the effect of the
karma manifests.[178]

Question: As Nāgārjuna's *Extensive Commentary on the Rice Seedling Sutra* states, this present self does not come from the former lifetime to this lifetime and does not transfer from this lifetime to the next. If this is so then this contradicts the Buddha's statement in the sutra that says, "I was at that time the universal ruler known as King Mahāsaṃmata." This is because the self of Mahāsaṃmata and the self of Śākyamuni would not be the same.

Answer: This sutra citation refutes the position that the Buddha and Mahāsaṃmata are two separate mental continua and just indicates that they share a single continuum. It does not show that the former and later selves of those two beings are the same. Moreover, the "I" in the phrase "I was at that time" does not mean a self that is permanent and established from its own side but means the mere "I" that is the basis of a conventional term. If you say also that this "I" is distinguished by a specific time, you are incorrect. The Buddha used it to mean the continuum of a mere general self that is not specified by time. Candrakīrti's *Clear Words* states:

> *Question*: A sutra states, "I was at that time the universal ruler known as King Mahāsaṃmata." How should we understand this statement?
>
> *Answer*: These words emphasize a refutation of their being totally separate and of their being one. Because of not being separate and not being one, at that time the Buddha was saying, "He [King Mahāsaṃmata] was not another [continuum] at the time."
>
> *Question*: What is wrong with saying, "That king is the Buddha," where the former and the present would be one?
>
> *Answer*: I have already indicated the fault when I said the self would be permanent.[179]

THE ABILITY TO POSIT A DEPENDENTLY EXISTING SELF WITHIN DEPENDENT ARISING

Therefore, when teaching the method of meditating on conventional dependent arising, the Buddha said in the *Rice Seedling Sutra*, "Depending on ignorance, conditioning factors arise" and so on, and, "Likewise, with the cessation of ignorance, conditioning factors cease" and so forth.

Through this, you respectively understand the way of meditating on afflictive dependent arising and purified dependent arising. When the Buddha taught the way of meditating on ultimate dependent arising, he stated in the *Rice Seedling Sutra*:

> Reverend Śāriputra, whoever, by means of perfect discriminating insight, sees this dependent arising perfectly taught by the Blessed One accordingly—in reality, continuous in perpetuity, without life [i.e., a self], free of life, just as it is, unerring, unborn, unarisen, not made, unconditioned, unobstructed, baseless, peaceful, fearless, not to be taken away, not exhausted, as an essential nature that is not pacified—and regards it as nonexistent, trifling, hollow, without essence, diseased, infected, a thorn, evil, impermanent, suffering, empty, and selfless, he does not reflect upon the past: Did I exist in the past or did I not exist in the past? What was I in the past? How was I in the past? He does not reflect upon the future: Will I exist in the future or not exist in the future? In the future what will I become? In the future how will I exist?

From thus understanding the way to meditate on conventional and ultimate dependent arising, you recognize a self that is a mere imputation in dependence on the aggregates and that passes through cyclic existence by means of true sufferings and true sources. You also see that there is a mere self that attains liberation by means of true paths and true cessations. However, you understand that there is no permanent self that is an entity separate from the aggregates, such as the non-Buddhists assert. Also, you understand that there is no self ultimately established from its own side, such as the Buddhist essentialists assert. You then eliminate all wrong philosophical views conceiving a permanent self that is an entity other than the aggregates or a self that is ultimately established from its own side, thinking that such a current self existed or did not exist in the past, or will exist or will not exist at some point in the future. You then have conviction in karmic causality and dependent arising and become skilled in traveling the path of selflessness.

The *Meeting of the Father and Son Sutra* clearly and definitively states:

> Great King, this "person" or "being" [depends on an aggregation
> of] the six elements, the six sense-bases of contact, the eighteen
> mental activities . . . [180]

Just as in this statement, the self of Dharmadatta, for instance, is imputed as
"self" in dependence on its basis of imputation: the six elements, which are
the four physical elements of earth, water, air, and fire along with the element of consciousness and the element of empty space (such as the space
inside the nostrils); the six sense-bases, from the eye sense-base to the mental sense-base; and the phenomena of the mind and mental processes, such
as the feeling created by visual contact.

Candrakīrti further states in his *Entering the Middle Way* (6.138–39):

> The Sage taught that the self is dependent
> on the six elements—earth, water, fire,
> wind, consciousness, and space—and on the
> six supports for contact—the eye and so on.
>
> He taught with certainty that you apprehend
> the phenomena of mind and mental processes.
> Therefore the self is neither them nor any one of these,
> either individually or collectively.

Consequently, by searching in the seven ways—same as the aggregates,
different from the aggregates, and so on—you do not find the self, and it
does not exist.[181] However, when you do not investigate or analyze, a convention of the world does exist. We impute "this is the self" in dependence on these aggregates, and the mode of the existence of the self is
accomplished by mere imputation in dependence on the aggregates. In
this way, we assert a self. Accordingly, Candrakīrti's *Entering the Middle
Way* (6.158) states:

> The chariot is not established in the seven ways,
> either in reality or for the world.
> Yet without analysis, just for the world,
> it is imputed in dependence on its parts.

Also, the same text states (6.150): "This is established in dependence on the aggregates." Candrakīrti's *Explanation of Entering the Middle Way* elaborates on this point:

> "This arises in dependence on that." We assert just this because it does not negate the presentation of conventional truths. However, there is no production from no cause, [no production from self, no production from other, and no production from both self and other]. Accordingly, if there is, in addition, genuine dependence on dependent imputation, it eliminates the faulty aspects just explained. You can then assert mere "imputation in dependence on the aggregates," because it affirms the conventions of the world, for you can witness the conventional imputation of the self. In order to establish the self as a mere imputation, I give an example of an external object and explain it because it clarifies the point just mentioned:
>
> > Similarly, a chariot is neither asserted to be other
> >   than its parts
> > nor to be non-other. It does not possess them.
> > It does not depend on the parts, and the parts do not
> >   depend on it.
> > Neither is it the mere collection of the parts, nor is it
> >   their shape.[182]

Consequently, phenomena such as the self, chariots, and so forth are established by mere imputation in dependence on their parts and bases of imputation. However, if you do not understand that their manner of existence is encompassed by mere dependent imputation, are not satisfied with just this, and look for an essence of the self, chariot, and so on, you will not find (1) a self that is the same as the aggregates or a chariot that is the same as its parts. Also, you will not find (2) a self or chariot that is separate from these. Accordingly, you do not find (3) a self or chariot that possesses its basis of imputation in terms of being exactly the same entity or that possesses its basis of imputation while being completely separate. Also, you do not find (4) a self or chariot that exists in the manner of the support that is categorically different from the basis of imputation or (5) in the manner of the supported that is categorically different from such. You do not find (6) a self or chariot that is the collection of its basis of imputation, nor do you find or establish (7) a chariot or self that is the shape of the chariot or body.

Question: When you search for phenomena in the seven ways and so forth, there does not exist an essence to anything. In that case, the conventions of self or chariot are not feasible. These conventions are well known in the world. As self, chariot, and so forth must exist, how do they exist?

Answer: This fault belongs to the essentialists. Essentialists posit things as existent and established after having examined and searched for them. When essentialists analyze and search for the self, chariots, and so forth, nothing can possibly exist, for they do not assert this method of establishing phenomena by mere dependent imputation without analysis.

We Mādhyamikas do not incur this fault. We assert that when you analyze and search for the self, chariot, and so on, you do not establish anything. Yet, without analyzing, we impute "self" or "chariot" in dependence on its aggregates or parts. These things are established by mere imputation in this way. In this vein, Candrakīrti's *Entering the Middle Way* (6.158) states:

> The chariot is not established in the seven ways,
> either in reality or for the world.
> Yet without analysis, just for the world,
> it is imputed in dependence on its parts.

At this point, Candrakīrti's *Explanation of Entering the Middle Way* states:

> When you search for a chariot in the seven ways—this method of considering, "A chariot is neither asserted to be other than its parts" and so forth—the chariot is not established either ultimately or conventionally. Nevertheless, you forego analysis, and in the world you impute a wheel and so forth on the basis of its parts, just as you do with blue and the like or a feeling and the like. This is because we assert dependent imputation just as we assert this mere conditionality of dependent arising. In our system we are not subject to the consequence of denying the con-

ventions of the world. It would be suitable for our opponents to also assert this. In our system, not only do we establish very clearly the imputation of the convention "chariot" in terms of its renown in the world, but we also assert without analysis any nominal attribute in terms of its renown in the world.

Consequently, if a phenomenon such as a self, a chariot, and so on inherently existed, then when you searched for it with analysis and were able to identify it, saying, "This is it," it would necessarily exist, but phenomena do not exist in this way. They exist by renown, without any analysis. From examining in these two ways—not finding the imputed object under analysis and existing by convention without analysis—yogis quickly fathom the depths of reality. Thus it is said that you must certainly assert in this way phenomena's mode of emptiness and mode of existence. Candrakīrti's *Entering the Middle Way* (6.160) states:

> "What does not exist in the seven ways—how could it exist?"
> Thinking this, yogis do not find the existence of the chariot
> and thereby easily enter into reality as well;
> hence, you also should assert the establishment of the chariot
>   in that way.

Candrakīrti's *Explanation of Entering the Middle Way* explains:

> For the yogi who is analyzing, if some inherently existent thing called "chariot" were to exist, then, without a doubt, wouldn't he find the existence of an essence by any of those seven ways? Yet no such thing is found. Therefore, thinking, "The so-called chariot is only imputed by the impairment of ignorance's cataract. Inherent establishment does not exist," the yogi generates certain knowledge and also easily enters into reality. The phrase "as well" [in the above citation] means that conventionalities are not lost, so you should assert this chariot as being established through renown without analysis. The learned think, "This position is flawless and beneficial," and assert it without hesitation.[183]

Je Tsongkhapa's *Elucidation of the Intent* states:

> Therefore the way that the chariot is established in this Madhyamaka system is that you should assert, accordingly, establishment without analysis. Candrakīrti says that in the Madhyamaka system the learned think, "This position is flawless and beneficial," and assert it without hesitation. Hence, this Prāsaṅgika Madhyamaka system is without fault, and you should make these assertions your own. Do not ascribe fault to it by saying, "The Prāsaṅgika Madhyamaka system has no assertions."[184]

Therefore, in this Prāsaṅgika system when you search for the meaning imputed in an imputation of conventions by worldly persons, such as "This is a chariot. This is a person," you cannot find anything in the manner of saying, "This is it!" In his Madhyamaka commentary, the master Buddhapālita tells a story about applying the conventions of the world in accordance with how it is renowned in the world:

> For entertainment two villagers sat in a temple and began to look at the drawings. One of them said, "This figure carrying a trident in his hand is Nārāyaṇa. His companion observed, "The one carrying a wheel in his hand is Īśvara." Another person in the temple commented, "You have them in the reverse. The one who holds the trident is Īśvara. The one who holds the wheel is Nārāyaṇa." The two companions were then arguing about it, so they went before a nearby wanderer and made obeisance. They each told him their thoughts about the identity of the drawings. The wanderer said to one of them, "Your statement [that the one with the trident] is Īśvara is true. To the other he said, "Your statement that [the one with the wheel in his hand is Īśvara] is untrue." Here, the wanderer knew that in reality there was no Īśvara in the temple, nor was Nārāyaṇa there. He knew that these were drawings on the wall. Yet, due to the power of worldly convention, he stated, "What this person says is true." This does not incur the fault of telling a lie.

Likewise, the Blessed One [Buddha] saw that things are empty of essential existence. Yet, due to the power of worldly convention he stated, "This is correct. This is incorrect."[185]

The Buddha is saying that you must understand how phenomena exist by mere imputation of conventions. In the *Heart Sutra*, the Buddha says that there is no form, no sound, and so on, saying that all phenomena—the aggregates, the constituents, and the sense-bases—do not exist. However, you must understand them to not exist intrinsically. It would be unsuitable to understand form and so on to be generally nonexistent. Likewise, you should also understand the self or person in this same way—as not existing intrinsically.

Dedication

By the two collections of merit and sublime wisdom attained through
reflecting a little on the Dharma's method of dependent arising,
as well as writing about it, explaining it, and worshiping its teacher,
may all beings attain the supreme two embodiments.

By the virtue of studying, reflecting, and meditating a little
on the Dharma's method of being unbiased toward the Conqueror's
    teachings in the Land of Snow,
may the Conqueror's teachings of the Land of Snow remain for a long
    time,
and may the Snowy Land's protector, His Holiness the Fourteenth
    Dalai Lama, Tenzin Gyatso, live a long time.

Notes

1. Most editions of the Kangyur here omit the phrase "he is enlightened" (*byang chub byed pa*), but it is present in the Dunhuang text Pelliot tibétain 551. Because Kamalaśīla comments upon the phrase, I have retained it.
   "Learner" refers to those on the first four of the five paths and "learned" to those on the fifth path, arhats and buddhas who have no further learning.
2. Dunhuang manuscript I translated at the British Library, Stog Palace, and Toyo Bunko manuscripts have "body" (*lus*) here, not after "firmness."
3. Same issue as before regarding placement of *lus*.
4. Non-Buddhist philosophers have a variety of explanations of production. Except for one system that says there is no cause for production, all the others have some form of permanent creator principle, whether it is "time," a principal nature, or a divine creator. For instance, some assert that time is permanent. When you feel sleepy, time produced this. Time also makes you then fall asleep and later wake up. Thus they say that everything is produced by time.
5. "Ignorance" here refers to the first of the twelve factors of dependent arising and is the apprehension of true existence. This apprehension gives rise to attachment and hostility, which then lead to conditioning factors, the second factor. Therefore, ignorance has the capacity to cause conditioning factors. The twelve factors are explained in more detail in chapters 6 and 7 below.
6. *Pratītyasamutpādādivibhaṅganirdeśa Sūtra*, 123b3.
7. *Yod pa nyid la sogs pa'i bye brag rnam par 'byed pa zhes bya ba'i chos kyi rnam grangs pa'i mdo*. This citation is found in Vasubandhu's *Explaining the First Factor of Dependent Arising and Its Divisions* (*Pratītyasamutpādādivibhaṅganirdeśa*), 5a4.
8. *Śālistambakakārikā*, 18b5.
9. *Śālistambakasūtraṭīkā*, 24b3.
10. Consequentialists here are those who propound the view of the Prāsaṅgika Madhymaka school of Buddhist philosophy. Essentialists in this context are those Buddhists philosophers who say an ultimate analysis can isolate some sort of intrinsic identity of objects. Prāsaṅgikas attribute essentialist views to the other Buddhist schools, such as Cittamātra and Vaibhāṣika.
11. The four valid cognitions (*pramāṇa*) are perceptual cognition, inferential cognition, analogy, and verbal testimony. See the discussion below on pages 78–79.
12. *Prasannapadā*, 25b5.
13. *Buddhapālitamūlamadhyamakavṛtti*, 206b7

14. *Ratnaguṇasañcayagāthā*, 11b4.
15. *Ratnaguṇasañcayagāthāpañjikā*, 53a2.
16. *Catuḥśatakaṭīkā*, 190b2.
17. The eight substances are the four elements—earth, water, fire, and wind—and the four substances arisen from them—form, smell, taste, and tangible substance. Sound is not included as it was not thought to involve material particles.
18. *Vigrahavyāvartanī*, 29a6.
19. *Prasannapadā*, 109a7.
20. *Suhṛllekha*, 45b7.
21. The Self-Existent Words are the non-Buddhist scriptures the Vedas. Those who follow the Vedas believe that they came into existence naturally without having been spoken by someone. If they were spoken, they would have faults.
22. *Tattvasaṅgraha*, 1a4.
23. *Tattvasaṅgraha*, 1a2.
24. *Tattvasaṅgraha*, 145a7.
25. Cited in the *Tattvasaṅgraha*, 142b1.
26. *Tattvasaṅgraha*, 3b3.
27. *Tattvasaṅgraha*, 3b3.
28. *Tattvasaṅgraha*, 4a3.
29. *Tattvasaṅgraha*, 3b4.
30. *Jñānagarbhasamuccayanāmanibandhana*, 37b1.
31. *Tattvasaṅgraha*, 3b5.
32. *Tattvasaṅgraha*, 3b5.
33. *Tattvasaṅgraha*, 4b5.
34. The pervasion would be: Anything that remains inert and then engages in effects is necessarily preceded by the will of a divine creator.
35. "Not different" in the sense of being like the creations in having shape, color, and so on and therefore being created by the will of a creator.
36. *Tattvasaṅgraha*, 4b1.
37. Momentary impermanence of any thing is a sequence of similar types of that thing. The thing seems the same over a period of time but is in fact different with each passing moment.
38. *Tattvasaṅgraha*, 7b2.
39. *Tattvasaṅgraha*, 7b4.
40. The idea here is that the effects that the creator made would sometimes work and sometimes not work, dependent on a variety of strategies.
41. Creating all at once would contradict the idea of play, where there are a variety of things going on constantly, sometimes working out and sometimes not working out.
42. *Tattvasaṅgraha*, 7b4.
43. *Tattvasaṅgraha*, 5a1.
44. "Unhindered" means that it will produce an effect in the next moment.
45. The idea here is the contrast with the way we experience things: an apple tree

gives fruit in the summer but not in the winter; bananas grow near the equator but not near the poles. If a creator has the total ability to be the sole cause, then we wouldn't observe such differences. Everything would be created everywhere at all times.

46. *Tattvasaṅgraha*, 8a1.

47. Fisherman in ancient India would only know how to catch fish and nothing else.

48. *Tattvasaṅgraha*, 8a1.

49. *Vinayakṣudrakavastu, tha*:242a6.

50. *Mahābalatantra*, 216b6.

51. Translation by Stephen Batchelor.

52. Nāgārjuna, *Sattvārādhana-gāthā*, 151a3. *Verses on Respecting Living Beings* was extracted from the *Tidal River Sutra* (*Ba tshwa'i chu klung gi mdo*) by Nāgārjuna. The sutra was never translated into Tibetan.

53. Nāgārjuna, *Sattvārādhana-gāthā*, 151b1.

54. Jinpa, *Wisdom of the Kadam Masters*, 62. *Sayings of the Kadam Masters* is the first work translated in the book *Wisdom of the Kadam Masters*.

55. *Siṅhanādikasūtra*, 121b1.

56. *Siṅhanādikasūtra*, 117a6.

57. *Abhidharmakośabhāṣya*, 128b7.

58. *Abhidharmakośaṭīkā*, 283a5.

59. *Abhidharmakośabhāṣya*, 129a1. A "functional thing" (*dngos po*) here means something that acts as a cause, bringing about an effect.

60. *Prasannapadā*, 64b3.

61. As quoted by Candrakīrti in *Clear Words*, 299b7.

62. *Catuḥśatakaṭīkā*, 207a4.

63. *Śatasāhasrikāprajñāpāramitā Sūtra*, 448b4.

64. *Catuḥśatakaṭīkā*, 133a6.

65. *Legs bshad snying po*, 143.

66. *Yuktiṣaṣṭikā*, verses 40–41.

67. *Illuminating Samsara and Nirvana*, 423.

68. *Stong thun chen mo*, 126a5. In other words, the other philosophical systems have a basic understanding of cause and effect—for example, that seeds give rise to sprouts.

69. *Illuminating Clearly*, 419.

70. *Chariot of Siddhas*, 71b1.

71. See *Rice Seedling Sutra* citation on page 15.

72. As quoted by Candrakīrti in *Clear Words*, 299b7.

73. *Lokātītastava*, 69a7.

74. *Śālistambakakārikā*, 18b5.

75. *Chariot of Siddhas*, 262.

76. *Chariot of Siddhas*, 263.

77. *Chariot of Siddhas*, 259.

78. *Chariot of Siddhas*, 262 and 264.

79. *Chariot of Siddhas*, 72.

80. *Flawless Garland of Candrakīrti's Words*, 100 and 106.

81. *Klu sgrub dgongs rgyan*, 157.

82. *Mountain Doctrine*, 102, 170, and 216.

83. *Illuminating Clearly*, 422–23.

84. *Samādhirāja Sūtra*, 174a4.

85. *Samādhirāja Sūtra*, 174b1.

86. *Catuḥśatakaṭīkā*, 224b3.

87. When something appears to us, it is not necessarily noticed and apprehended. If we are looking at a panorama of appearances from the top of a mountain, for instance, we don't apprehend everything that appears to us.

88. *Catuḥśatakaṭīkā*, 175b2.

89. *Catuḥśatakaṭīkā* on 13.21.

90. Candrakīrti, *Catuḥśatakaṭīkā* on 13.11.

91. Candrakīrti, *Catuḥśatakaṭīkā* on 15.10.

92. The "basis, path, and goal" is a common framework for presenting Buddhist practice. The basis is conventional truths and ultimate truths. Conventional truths are forms, sounds, smells, and so on, and their emptiness of intrinsic existence comprises ultimate truths. On this basis you cultivate the path of method and wisdom. Method is things like love, compassion, and the altruistic spirit of enlightenment that is preoccupied with others rather than oneself. Wisdom is the wisdom that knows emptiness, impermanence, suffering, and the like. Based on these, you respectively attain the goal of a buddha's embodiment of form (*rūpakāya*) and a buddha's truth embodiment (*dharmakāya*). The form embodiment includes a buddha's distinct physical features, the realm in which he or she abides, and so on. The truth embodiment includes the abandonment of all defilements and the attainment of omniscience.

93. *Catuḥśatakaṭīkā*, 258b7.

94. *Prasannapadā*, 23a3.

95. As noted above, these seven analyze the relation between an object and its parts. The analysis shows that (1) an object is not other than its parts, (2) an object is not *not* other than its parts, (3) an object does not possess its parts, (4) an object does not depend on its parts, and (5) the parts do not depend on the object. Finally, an object is neither (6) the mere collection of its parts nor (7) their shape.

96. *Madhyamakāvatārabhāṣya* at 6.158.

97. *Prasannapadā*, 9a2.

98. *Prajñāpāramitāhṛdaya Sūtra*, 78a1.

99. *Paramārthaśūnyatā Sūtra*, as quoted in the *Madhyamakāvatārabhāṣya*. See the quotation of same passage (with a slight variance in the Tibetan) by Vasubandhu in his *Presentation of Reason* below on page 130.

100. *Prajñāpāramitāhṛdaya Sūtra*, 77.6.

101. *Śatasāhasrikāprajñāpāramitā Sūtra*, 448b4.

102. *Catuḥśatakaṭīkā*, 207a4.

103. *Samādhirāja Sūtra*, 26b5.
104. *Samādhirāja Sūtra*, 26b6.
105. To be "established by way of own characteristics" (Tib. *rang gi mtshan nyid kyis grub pa*) is how the Prāsaṅgikas describe the view of the Svātantrika-Madhyamaka school, to which they ascribe the subtlest form of essentialism. As Mādhyamikas, Svātantrikas follow Nāgārjuna in refuting self-existence (*svabhāva*), but they still cling to conventionally real phenomena as retaining some subtler "character" or "own characteristics" (*svalakṣana*) that makes them suitable to be identified in each phenomenon's particular way. But holding to even such a subtle character undermines the truth of dependent arising. For the Prāsaṅgikas, all such descriptions are synonymous with being "established by intrinsic existence" or being "established from its own side."
106. *Laṅkāvatāra Sūtra*, 174b5.
107. *Madhyamakāvatārabhāṣya*, 205a5.
108. *Madhyamakāvatārabhāṣya*, 256a2.
109. Perceptual and inferential each have both conventional and ultimate objects. Analogy and verbal testimony have conventional objects and are inferential.
110. *Catuḥśatakaṭīkā*, 197b5.
111. *Vigrahavyāvartanī*, 27a4.
112. *Prasannapadā*, 25b5.
113. *Prasannapadā*, 25b5.
114. *Great Treatise*, 3:178.
115. See section "Dependently Arisen Production Is Actual Production" above.
116. *Abhiniṣkramaṇa Sūtra*, 66a3.
117. *Abhiniṣkramaṇa Sūtra*, 66a5.
118. *Vinayavibhaṅga*, 114a2.
119. There are four stages: death, intermediate state, birth (which refers to conception), and the stage of existence, which lasts from birth to death.
120. *Book of Kadam*, section 5, 727. See alternate translation in Jinpa, *Book of Kadam*, 197.
121. As the commentary states, this drawing is included to symbolize transience and not to represent the deity Yama.
122. *Vinayavibhaṅga*, 115a2.
123. "Undertake" is from the two verses above. This begins a word commentary on those verses.
124. The *Dependent Arising Sutra*, which in its most condensed version consists of one verse, is called *Ye Dharma* because the Sanskrit rendering of this verse begins with this phrase. Among its various names mentioned in this text, it is also commonly known as the *Essence of Dependent Arising Sutra* (*Rten 'brel snying po'i mdo*).
125. *Pratītyasamutpāda Sūtra*, 125b2.
126. *Pratītyasamutpāda Sūtra*, 125b3.
127. This world system is called Tolerable (*mi mjed*, Skt. *sahā*) in that the beings herein "tolerate" or "put up with" manifold forms of suffering. As His Holiness the Dalai

Lama explains: "Buddhist texts call our world the 'tolerable world,' since we have access to the antidote to mistaking the nature of self, and therefore have no need to fear afflictive emotions; this allows us to tolerate being in such a bad state." Dalai Lama, *Becoming Enlightened*, 63.

128. The Brahmā worlds are the first three of the seventeen heavens of the form-realm gods. The pure abodes are the five highest heavens of the form-realm gods.

129. In its present form, Dhamek Stupa is very large, but the original stupa from the time of King Aśoka was quite a bit smaller. When the stupa was made larger, the builders inserted the inscription of the *Dependent Arising Sutra*.

130. Agrawala, *Archaeological Survey of India*, 11.

131. Upasak, *Nalanda: Past and Present*, 55.

132. *Abhiniṣkramaṇa Sūtra*, 58a7.

133. The four fearlessnesses are fearlessness of (1) asserting his own perfect realization, (2) asserting his own perfect abandonment, (3) giving the teaching on obstructions, and (4) indicating the path of certain emergence.

134. In other words, (1) the suffering of obvious pain, (2) the suffering of change, which refers to the transience of pleasant experiences, and (3) the suffering of pervasive conditioning, which is the way all our actions, driven by ignorance, keep us locked in the cycle of suffering existence.

135. Non-Buddhists say that something that is permanent can produce an effect and is therefore functioning. Buddhists say that only impermanent things can produce an effect.

136. *Śālistambakasūtraṭīkā*, 29b3.

137. *Sphuṭārthā*, 130a6.

138. *Samādhirāja Sūtra*, 41a1.

139. The four types of sutras interpretable based on context are those that intend (1) a meaning of equality, (2) another meaning, (3) another time, and (4) a person's thought. The four types of circuitous intention sutras are (1) induction, (2) character, (3) antidote, and (4) transformation. "Equality" here means, for instance, when the Buddha says that he was a certain buddha, it is because all buddhas are equal in (1) having completed the two collections of method and sublime wisdom, (2) having attained the truth embodiment, and (3) working for the welfare of all living beings. According to the Prasaṅgika Madhyamaka school, who assert that *all* phenomena are empty of existence by self-characteristics, "circuitous intention of character" means, for instance, how the Buddha taught the third turning of the wheel of Dharma. Therein he divided phenomena into three natures: imputational, dependent, and perfected, and said the first is empty of being established by self-characteristics and the other two are established by self-characteristics.

140. *Śālistambakaṭīkā*, 154a4.

141. *Śālistambakaṭīkā*, 154a5.

142. *Śālistambakaṭīkā*, 178b8.

143. *Mahāyānasaṅgraha*, 66b5.

144. *Viniścayasaṅgrahaṇī*, 250b5.

145. *Dri ba lhag bsam rab dkar*, 137.
146. *Lam rim nyams mgur*, vv. 18–19.
147. *Śālistambakaṭīkā*, 178b8.
148. *Śālistambakaṭīkā*, 178b2.
149. *Pratītyasamutpādādivibhaṅganirdeśa*, 54b2.
150. *Pratītyasamutpādādivibhaṅganirdeśa*, 54b1. This means that cause and effect would be destroyed together, and there would not be the succession of destruction that is part of the idea of momentariness.
151. The reason that the selflessness of persons is described here as being the lack of a substantially established person (*gang zag gi rdzas yod kyis stong pa*) rather than the lack of an inherently existent person is that this paragraph explains the meaning of the Kamalaśīla citation that follows it. Kamalaśīla was from the Svātantrika Madhyamaka school, which asserts the selflessness of persons to be the lack of a substantially established person. The Prasaṅgika Mādhyamaka school asserts it to be the lack of an inherently existent person.
152. When you ingest medicine, it gradually eliminates your illness. In the same way, you cultivate the wisdom that knows emptiness, and this gradually ceases ignorance and the other factors of dependent arising, one by one. This pill is to increase your strength and thereby help you to live longer.
153. *Śālistambakaṭīkā*, 178b5.
154. See translation, 1:320.
155. *Śālistambakaṭīkā*, 179a2.
156. As the text notes below, *projecting* is used because it is from far away. *Actualizing* is used because it is right nearby.
157. For birth in a human mother's womb, *birth* refers to conception. *Name-and-form*, *sources*, *contact*, and *feeling* in the beginning refer to the development of the embryo. Therefore, between birth and aging and death are the projected factors of name-and-form, sources, contact, and feeling. When name-and-form, sources, contact, and feeling are mentioned, birth and aging and death are also understood to occur. Craving, grasping, and becoming are mostly understood as those that occur in the moments before death.
158. *Abhidharmasamuccaya*, 65b3. Here Asaṅga expresses the position of the "upper" Abhidharma school of the Yogācāra. There are both a lower Abhidharma [Vaibhāṣika] and an upper Abhidharma [Cittamātra].
159. "Occasion dependent arising" (*rten 'brel gnas bskabs pa*) states that with each factor of dependent arising, you have to assert that all five aggregates are present. For instance, when you state, "the dependent arising factor of ignorance," you must posit the presence of all five aggregates. The other schools of Buddhist thought do not state that the twelve factors must be understood in this way.
160. *Lakṣaṇānusāriṇī*, 286b4.
161. *Yogācārabhūmi*, 117b3.
162. This is the state called *mer mer po*. The eyes, nose, ears, and other sense faculties

form, and based on these, the sensory consciousnesses are able to arise. However, consciousness is not clear at this point.

163. *Yogācārabhūmi*, 19a1.

164. *Abhidharmakośabhāṣya*, 131a1.

165. *Śālistambakaṭīkā*, 191a3.

166. Birth stage is the immediate moment of birth.

167. This is a line from Nāgārjuna's *Verses on the Rice Seedling Sutra*, the root text for his *Extensive Commentary on the Rice Seedling Sutra*.

168. *Śālistambakasūtraṭīkā*, 39a3.

169. *Prasannapadā*, 192b4.

170. To be one nature (*ngo bo gcig*) means that self and the aggregates are inextricably related such that you can't have one without the other, like the fingers and the hand. To be different natures (*ngo bo gzhan*) means that they are unrelated like a tiger and a cow, like yellow and blue, which can be directly perceived as separate.

171. *Madhyamakāvatārabhāṣya*, 199b6.

172. *Śālistambakaṭīkā*, 187b2.

173. *Śālistambakaṭīkā*, 194a4.

174. *Pratītyasamutpādahṛdaya*, v. 5.

175. *Vyākhyāyukti*, 109b4. Vasubandhu explains the seeming problem in the Buddha's statement from sutra as indicating that karma and maturation exist substantially whereas the person (here "agent") exists imputationally.

176. *Viśeṣastava*, 3b7.

177. *Śālistambakakārikā*, 20a3.

178. *Śālistambakasūtraṭīkā*, 48b7. The sense of the question is that if there is nothing that comes from the previous life to this life or goes from this life to the next, don't you have to explain the transition from one life to the next by proposing a permanent self, no cause, or a discordant cause?

179. *Prasannapadā*, 191a7.

180. *Pitāputrasamāgama Sūtra*, 127b3. The eighteen mental activities are the three sets of feelings—pleasurable, painful, and neutral—that arise from the six contacts associated with the six sense-bases.

181. For the seven ways, see note 95 above and page 139.

182. *Madhyamakāvatārabhāṣya* at 6.151, 303b6.

183. *Madhyamakāvatārabhāṣya*, 306a5.

184. *Dbu ma dgongs pa rab gsal*, 220b5.

185. *Buddhapālitamūlamadhyamakavṛtti*, 244b3.

Bibliography

Agrawala, V. S. *Archaeological Survey of India*. 3rd ed. New Delhi: Director General, Archaeological Survey of India, 1980.

Āryadeva. *Four Hundred Stanzas. Catuḥśataka*. Derge Tengyur (Toh 3846), dbu ma, tsha.

Asaṅga. *Compendium of Determinations. Viniścayasaṅgrahaṇī*. Derge Tengyur (Toh 4038), sems tsam, zhi and zi.

———. *Compendium of Knowledge. Abhidharmasamuccaya*. Derge Tengyur (Toh 4049), sems tsam, ri.

———. *Compendium of the Mahayana. Mahāyānasaṅgraha*. Derge Tengyur (Toh 4048), sems tsam, ri.

———. *Yogic Levels. Yogācārabhūmi*. Derge Tengyur (Toh 4035–37), sems tsam, tshi–wi.

Bodhibhadra. *Explanation of Jñānagarbha's Compendium of the Essence of Wisdom. Jñānagarbhasamuccayanāmanibandhana*. Derge Tengyur (Toh 3852), dbu ma, tsha.

Book of Kadam. Bka' gdams glegs bam, 2 vols. Xining: Mtsho sngon mi rigs dpe skrun khang, 1993–94.

Buddhapālita. *Buddhapālita's Commentary on Fundamental Verses of the Middle Way. Buddhapālitamūlamadhyamakavṛtti*. Derge Tengyur (Toh 3842), dbu ma, tsa.

Candrakīrti. *Clear Words. Prasannapadā*. Derge Tengyur (Toh 3860), dbu ma, 'a.

———. *Commentary on the Four Hundred Stanzas. Catuḥśatakaṭīkā*. Derge Tengyur (Toh 3865), dbu ma, ya.

———. *Entering the Middle Way. Madhyamakāvatāra*. Derge Tengyur (Toh 3861), dbu ma, 'a.

———. *Explanation of Entering the Middle Way. Madhyamakāvatārabhāṣya*. Derge Tengyur (Toh 3862), dbu ma, 'a.

Collection of Aphorisms. Udānavarga. Derge Kangyur (Toh 326), mdo sde, sa.

Dalai Lama, His Holiness the. *Becoming Enlightened*. Translated and edited by Jeffrey Hopkins. New York: Atria, 2009.

Dependent Arising Sutra. Pratītyasamutpāda Sūtra. Derge Kangyur (Toh 212), mdo sde, tsha.

Descent to Laṅkā Sutra. Laṅkāvatāra Sūtra. Derge Kangyur (Toh 107), mdo sde, ca.

Dharmakīrti. *Commentary on Valid Cognition. Pramāṇavārttika*. Derge Tengyur (Toh 4210), tshad ma, ce.

Dolpopa Sherab Gyatso. *Mountain Doctrine: An Ocean of Definitive Meaning. Ri chos nges don rgya mtsho*. New Delhi: Institute of Tibetan Classics, 2013.

Exegesis of the Discipline. Vinayavibhaṅga. Derge Kangyur (Toh 3), 'dul ba, *ca.*

Finer Points of Discipline. Vinayakṣudrakavastu. Derge Kangyur (Toh 6), 'dul ba, *tha* and *da.*

Gendun Chophel. *Dhammapada. Chos kyi tshigs su cad pa'i mdo.* Translated from the Pali. New Delhi: T. G. Dhongthog, 1976.

———. *Ornament to the Intent of Nāgārjuna: An Elegant Inquiry into the Profound Points of Madhyamaka. Dbu ma'i zab gnad snying por dril ba'i legs bshad klu sgrub dgongs rgyan.* Gsung 'bum of Dge 'dun chos 'phel, 2:71–156. Chengdu: Sichuan People's Printing Press (Si khron mi rigs dpe skrun khang), 2009.

Gorampa. *Illuminating Samsara and Nirvana: A Presentation of Dependent Arising. Rten 'brel gyi rnam par bzhag pa 'khor 'das rab gsal. Go rams pa gsung 'bum. The Collected Works of Kun-mkhyen Go-rams-pa Bsod-nams-seng-ge,* 8:395–459. Dehradun: Sakya College, 1979.

Haribhadra. *Clarification of the Meaning Commentary. Sphuṭārthā.* Derge Tengyur (Toh 3793), shes phyin, *ja.*

———. *Commentary on the Verse Summary Sutra. Ratnaguṇasañcayagāthāpañjikā.* Derge Tengyur (Toh 3792), shes phyin, *ja.*

———. *Illumination of the Ornament for Realizations. Abhisamayālaṅkārāloka.* Derge Tengyur (Toh 3791), sher phyin, *cha.*

Heart Sutra. Prajñāpāramitāhṛdaya Sūtra. Derge Kangyur (Toh 531), rgyud, *na*:94b1–95b3.

Jinpa, Thupten, trans. *The Book of Kadam: The Core Texts.* Somerville: Wisdom Publications, 2008.

———. *Wisdom of the Kadam Masters.* Somerville: Wisdom Publications, 2013.

Kamalaśīla. *Compendium of Reality Commentary. Tattvasaṅgrahapañjikā.* Derge Tengyur (Toh 4267), tshad ma, *ze.*

———. *Detailed Commentary on the Rice Seedling Sutra. Śālistambakaṭīkā.* Peking Tengyur, mdo 'grel, *ji.*

Karmapa Mikyö Dorje. *Chariot of Siddhas of the Dakpo Kagyu: An Extended Commentary on the Madhyamakāvatāra. Dbu ma la 'jug pa'i rnam bshad dpal ldan dus gsum mkhyen pa'i zhal lung dwags brgyud grub pa'i shing rta.* Dpal spungs gdan sa 'khyil.

Khedrup Je. *Dose of Emptiness. Stong thun chen mo.* Tsang edition.

King of Concentration Sutra. Samādhirāja Sūtra. Derge Kangyur (Toh 127), mdo sde, *da.*

Maitreya. *Ornament of the Sutras. Sūtrālaṅkāra.* Derge Tengyur (Toh 4020), sher phyin, *phi.*

———. *Sublime Continuum. Uttaratantra.* Derge Tengyur (Toh 4024), sems tsam, *phi.*

Meeting of the Father and Son Sutra. Pitāputrasamāgamana Sūtra. Derge Kangyur (Toh 60), dkon brtsegs, *nga.*

Mipham. *Flawless Garland of Candrakīrti's Words: A Commentary on the Madhyamakāvatāra. Dbu ma la 'jug pa'i 'grel ba zla ba'i zhal lung dri med shel phreng.* Gangtok, Sikkim: Sonam Topgay Kazi, 1979.

Nāgārjuna. *Dispelling Debates. Vigrahavyāvartanī.* Derge Tengyur (Toh 3828), dbu ma, *tsa.*

———. *Essence of Dependent Arising. Pratītyasamutpādahṛdaya.* Derge Tengyur (Toh 3836), dbu ma, *tsa.*

———. *Extensive Commentary on the Rice Seedling Sutra. Śālistambakasūtraṭīkā.* Derge Tengyur (Toh 3986), mdo 'grel, *ngi.*

———. *Friendly Letter. Suhṛllekha.* Derge Tengyur (Toh 4182), spring yig, *nge.*

———. *Fundamental Verses on the Middle Way.* Mūlamadhyamakakārikā. Derge Tengyur (Toh 3824), dbu ma, *tsa.*

———. *Hymn to the World Transcendent. Lokātītastava.* Derge Tengyur (Toh 1120), bstod tshogs, *ka.*

———. *Praise of the Inconceivable. Acintyastava.* Derge Tengyur (Toh 1128), bstod tshogs, *ka.*

———. *Precious Garland. Ratnāvalī.* Derge Tengyur (Toh 4158), spring yig, *ge.*

———. *Sixty Stanzas of Reasoning. Yuktiṣaṣṭikā.* Derge Tengyur (Toh 3825), dbu ma, *tsa.*

———. *Verses on Respecting Living Beings. Sattvārādhana-gāthā.* Peking Tengyur, mdo 'grel, *gi.*

———. *Verses on the Rice Seedling Sutra. Śālistambakakārikā.* Derge Tengyur (Toh 3985), mdo 'grel, *ngi.*

Perfection of Wisdom Sutra in 100,000 Verses. Śatasāhasrikāprajñāpāramitā Sūtra. Lhasa Kangyur, 'bum, *na.*

Perfect Renunciation Sutra. Abhiniṣkramaṇa Sūtra. Derge Kangyur (Toh 301), mdo sde, *sa.*

Pūrṇavardhana. *Following the Definitions. Lakṣaṇānusāriṇī.* Derge Tengyur (Toh 4093), mngon pa, *cu* and *chu.*

Rice Seedling Sutra. Śālistāmba Sūtra. Sā lu ljang pa'i mdo. Dunhuang PT 551, and Derge Kangyur (Toh 210), mdo sde, *tsha.*

Śāntarakṣita. *Compendium of Reality. Tattvasaṅgraha.* Derge Tengyur (Toh 4266), tshad ma, *ze.*

Śāntideva. *Engaging in the Bodhisattva's Deeds. Bodhicaryāvatāra.* Derge Tengyur (Toh 3871), dbu ma, *la.*

Shakya Chokden. *Illuminating Clearly the Garland of 108 Beads of Logical Mistakes in the Madhyamaka Systems of Others. Gzhan lugs kyi ni dbu ma la rtog ges brtags pa'i nor ba'i phrang brgya dang rtsa brgyad yod pa yi ngos 'dzin gsal po.* Gsung 'bum of Shākya mchog ldan, 4:415–27. Thimpu, Bhutan: Kunzang Tobgey, 1975.

Sutra Explaining the First Factor of Dependent Arising and Its Divisions. Pratītyasamutpādādināvibhaṅganirdeśa Sūtra. Derge Kangyur (Toh 211), mdo sde, *tsha.*

Sutra Proclaiming the Lion's Roar. Siṁhanādika Sūtra. Derge Kangyur, mdo sde, *tsha:*111b7–115b7.

Tantra of Very Powerful Glory. Mahābalatantra. Derge Kangyur (Toh 391), rgyud, *ga.*

Tsongkhapa. *Elucidation of the Intent. Dbu ma dgongs pa rab gsal.* Lhasa edition. Zhol Press.

———. *Essence of Eloquence. Legs bshad snying po.* Tsang edition.

———. *Great Treatise on the Stages of the Path to Enlightenment. Lam rim chen mo.* English translation by the Lamrim Chenmo Translation Committee, 3 vols. Ithaca, NY: Snow Lion Publications, 2000–2004.

———. *Praise of Dependent Arising. Rten 'brel bstod pa.* In *Chos spyod zhal 'don nyer mkho phyogs bsdebs*, 79ff. Sarnath: Gelugpa Students Welfare Committee, 1987.

———. *Questions with Virtuous High Resolve. Dri ba lhag bsam rab dkar. Tsong kha pa'i bka' 'bum thor bu.* Xining: Mtsho sngon mi rigs dpe skrun khang, 1987.

———. *Songs of Experience. Lam rim nyams mgur.* In *Chos spyod zhal 'don nyer mkho phyogs bsdebs*, 64ff. Sarnath: Gelugpa Students Welfare Committee, 1987.

Udbhatasiddhasvamin. *Praise of the Exalted One. Viśeṣastava.* Derge Tengyur (Toh 1109), bstod tshogs, *ka.*

Upasak, Chandrika Singh, ed. *Nalanda: Past and Present.* Nalanda: Nava Nalanda Mahavihara, 1977.

Vasubandhu. *Explaining the First Factor of Dependent Arising and Its Divisions. Pratītyasamutpādādivibhaṅganirdeśa.* Derge Tengyur (Toh 3995), mdo 'grel, *chi.*

———. *Presentation of Reason. Vyākhyāyukti.* Derge Tengyur (Toh 4061), sems tsam, *shi.*

———. *Treasury of Knowledge Autocommentary. Abhidharmakośabhāṣya.* Derge Tengyur (Toh 4090), mngon pa, *ku.*

———. *Treasury of Knowledge. Abhidharmakośa.* Derge Tengyur (Toh 4089), mngon pa, *ku.*

Verse Summary Sutra. Ratnaguṇasañcayagāthā. Derge Kangyur (Toh 13), shes rab sna tshogs, *ka.*

Yaśomitra (Jinaputra). *Extensive Commentary on the Treasury of Knowledge. Abhidharmakośaṭīkā.* Derge Tengyur (Toh 4092), mngon pa, *gu.*

Index

A

action, independent, 22–23. *See also* virtuous or nonvirtuous actions
actualized, actualizing factors, 10, 121–23, 126
affliction. *See* cyclic existence
afflictive phenomena, 97, 109, 137, 149–50n127
aggregates, 8, 28, 31–32, 78, 125, 151n159
aging and death. *See* twelve-factor dependent arising
air element, 3–6, 24–25, 43
altruism, 32, 47, 51–52, 89–90, 96, 100, 148n92. *See also* compassion
annihilation, 4, 10–11, 58, 71–72, 131
ascetics, 11, 103
assertion, fearlessness of, 102
attachment, 7, 13, 49, 51, 92, 94, 105–7, 145n5. *See also* cyclic existence
attention, 9

B

basis, path, and goal, 75, 98, 104, 148n93
becoming, 2, 7–8, 95, 116, 121–23, 151n157. *See also* internal dependent arising; twelve-factor dependent arising
birth, 2, 5, 7–9, 115, 120–21, 125–26, 149n119. *See also* cyclic existence; twelve-factor dependent arising
body, 5–7, 78–79, 131, 135, 138. *See also* self: imputed

C

carriage. *See* chariot metaphor
cause and effect, 14–21, 23, 35. *See also*
cyclic existence; karma; twelve-factor dependent arising
causes, virtuous and nonvirtuous, 37
chariot metaphor, 22, 31, 57, 70–71, 76–77, 83–84, 130–31, 138–42
clear light mind, 51, 99
clinging, 62, 98. *See also* cyclic existence; twelve-factor dependent arising
cognition, valid, 23, 40–41, 44, 78–85, 145n1
compassion, 35–36, 41–42, 44–45, 51–52, 87–88, 89, 148n92. *See also* altruism
composite phenomena, 15–21, 25, 29, 33–34, 57, 59–63, 68, 74, 81, 118
conditioning factors, 1–2, 5–9, 93–94, 145n5. *See also* twelve-factor dependent arising
conflict, 2, 7, 113, 115–16
consciousness, 1–2, 5–10, 32, 36–37, 45, 60, 68–71, 78–84, 93, 121–26, 133, 151–52n162. *See also* twelve-factor dependent arising
consequentialists, 20, 26–27, 29, 145n10
contact, 1–2, 7–8, 94–95, 138, 151n157, 152n180. *See also* twelve-factor dependent arising
continuity of the similar, 4–5, 10–11
conventional dependent arising, meditating on, 114–15, 134–35, 137
craving, 2, 7–9, 94, 120–21. *See also* twelve-factor dependent arising
cyclic existence, 8, 28, 31–32, 92, 98, 104, 108, 114, 123. *See also* liberation; twelve-factor dependent arising

D

defilements, 8–10, 46, 51, 99, 148n92
dependent and linked arising, 15–22. *See also* cyclic existence; external dependent arising; internal dependent arising; twelve-factor dependent arising
Dependent Arising Sutra, 99–104, 107–8, 149n124
Dhamek Stupa, Sarnath, 101, 150n128
divine creator (Īśvara), 14–20, 33–38, 40–44, 50, 104, 142, 146–47n45, 146n34

E

ear, 78–79, 94–95, 138, 151–52n162
earth, 24–25
earth element, 3–4, 5–6, 43, 146n17
effort, study, 32, 35, 88, 136, 148n92. *See also* meditation practice
eightfold noble path, 2, 82, 98, 104, 109, 119. *See also* liberation
elements, 3–6, 24, 37–38, 40, 138
emptiness, 28–31, 99, 108. *See also* liberation; reality
erroneous mind, 69
essentialists, 20–21, 26–27, 29, 55–56, 61–62, 71–73, 75–76, 140, 145n10
eternalism, 4, 10, 29, 56, 58, 61, 69, 71–72, 96, 131
ethical behavior, discipline, 88–89
external dependent arising, 3–5, 17, 34, 55, 131
eye, 9, 73, 78–79, 94–95, 138, 151–52n162

F

fearlessnesses, four, 102–4, 150n133
feeling(s), 1–2, 7–8, 94, 120–22, 126, 151n157, 152n180
fire element, 3–4, 5–6
five aggregates. *See* aggregates
form embodiment, 9, 104, 148n93
four noble truths, 88–89, 92, 98, 104, 114–15. *See also* sublime wisdom truth; truth embodiment
function, 29
functional things, 14, 56, 74, 147n59
future lives. *See* cyclic existence; karma; rebirth

G

grasping, 2, 7–8, 94. *See also* twelve-factor dependent arising

H

happiness. *See* joy
Heart Sutra, 77–78, 141
helpfulness. *See* altruism
hostility, 13, 49, 51, 92, 105–7, 145n5

I

identity, 13–14, 20, 25–26. *See also* self: imputed
ignorance, 1–2, 5–9, 13, 49, 51, 92–94, 145n3, 145n5. *See also* cyclic existence; twelve-factor dependent arising
impermanence, 8, 19–20, 146n40
imputation, 13, 21–27, 30, 58, 67, 76–78, 139–41. *See also* mind; production, dependently risen vs. genuine
independent action, 22–23
independent causation/existence, 19–21, 26–29, 32, 58
interdependence, mutual dependence, 21, 23, 56–57, 67, 75, 83
internal dependent arising, 5–11, 55, 129–33
Īśvara. *See* divine creator (Īśvara)

J

joy, 14, 37–38, 51–52

K

karma, 7–11, 24–25, 32, 45–53, 92–97, 102–8, 114–16, 119–23, 134–35. *See also* cyclic existence; rebirth; twelve-factor dependent arising

L

liberation, 32–33, 36, 52–53, 87, 88–89, 96–98, 102–4, 109, 136, 148n92. *See also* merit; sublime wisdom truth

M

meditation practice, 2, 35, 47, 82, 109, 114–17
mental activities, 38, 88, 138, 152n180
mental sense-base, 78–79, 138

merit, 11, 52, 87–88, 100
method for attaining knowledge. *See*
  liberation
middle way, 29–31, 88. *See also* liberation;
  twelve-factor dependent arising
mind. *See* consciousness; imputation;
  internal dependent arising
misery, 7
moon metaphor, 10, 132–33

N

name-and-form, 1–2, 6–8, 94, 126. *See also*
  twelve-factor dependent arising
nature embodiment, 99–100
nihilism, 14, 29, 47, 74–76, 104
nirvāṇa, 2, 96, 104
noble path. *See* eightfold noble path; four
  noble truths
noncomposite/noncompounded phenomena, 21–22, 56
nonvirtuous deeds. *See* virtuous or nonvirtuous actions
nose, 78–79, 94–95, 138

O

objects, imputed, 14, 26–27, 30–32,
  57–59, 71, 73–74, 84, 99, 140–42
occasion dependent arising, 151n159
order of dependent arising, forward and
  reverse, 97, 113–17

P

partless particle, 15–16, 20, 26, 28, 35, 59,
  63
permanence. *See* eternalism
permanent causes, 14–17, 35. *See also*
  eternalism
person. *See* consciousness; identity; self:
  imputed
phenomena, composite, 15–17
play/playfulness, 42, 146n41
potter metaphor, 36, 46
potter simile, 93, 95
Prāsaṅgika Madhyamaka school, 23, 27, 29,
  66–67, 71, 73, 75–76, 78, 127, 142,
  145n10, 150n139, 151n151. *See also*
  consequentialists

production, dependently risen vs. genuine,
  63–74, 139, 145n4
projecting factors, 121–23, 151n157

R

reality, 7, 12, 28, 60, 67, 73, 81–84, 99,
  108–10, 140–42
realization, perfect, 103
rebirth, 7, 10, 11, 37, 46, 51, 87–88, 93,
  96, 108, 121–23, 131–32, 137. *See also*
  cyclic existence; karma; twelve-factor
  dependent arising
result, attainment of, 2, 4–5, 10–11. *See
  also* karma

S

season element, 3–4, 34, 43–44
self
  imputed, 106, 129, 134, 138
  separate, 13, 27–28, 31–32, 58, 61, 92,
    127–32, 137, 142
  See also person
Self-Existent Words, 33–34, 146n21. *See
  also* divine creator (Īśvara)
selflessness of persons and objects, 27–28,
  35–36, 100, 103, 108, 151n151
sense-bases, six, 1–2, 7–8, 94, 138
six elements. *See* elements
sorrow, sources, 2, 7, 14. *See also* internal
  dependent arising; twelve-factor dependent arising
space element, 3–6, 9–10, 21, 24–25, 56, 138
sublime wisdom truth, 32, 79, 87, 98–100,
  103–4, 110–11, 148n92, 150n139
substances, eight, 146n17
suffering, 14. *See also* cyclic existence;
  karma; twelve-factor dependent arising
sutras, types of, 150n139
Svātantrika-Madhyamaka school, 149n105,
  151n151

T

teachers, 48, 63, 91
things. *See* consciousness; production,
  dependently risen vs. genuine
time, 8–11, 14–20, 40, 50, 81, 89, 97, 104,
  108

tongue, 78–79, 94, 138, 151–52n162
transference, 10, 15, 131–36
transmigration, 4–5, 10–11, 127, 131–32
truth embodiment, 99–100, 104, 148n92,
    148n93
twelve-factor dependent arising, 8–9,
    13–20, 88–89, 92–96, 102–4, 113–18,
    120–24, 145n5. *See also* cyclic existence

U
ultimate dependent arising, meditating on,
    114–15, 137

V
virtuous or nonvirtuous actions, 22–23, 35,
    37–41, 45–50, 60, 77, 87–88, 92–94,
    96, 105–8
visual consciousness, 9–10, 79–80, 83

W
water element, 3–6, 24, 32, 43, 51, 138
wheel of life imagery, 91–97, 150n139. *See
    also* cyclic existence
wisdom. *See* four noble truths; sublime
    wisdom truth

About the Author

Professor Geshe Yeshe Thabkhe was born in 1930 in Lhokha, Central Tibet, and became a monk of Drepung Loseling Monastery at the age of thirteen. After completing his studies in 1969, Geshe Thabkhe was awarded the highest academic degree offered in the Geluk school of Tibetan Buddhism. Since 1972, he has served as professor of the Indian tradition of Buddhist philosophy at Central Institute of Higher Tibetan Studies, the only Tibetan university in India. He has also served as a lecturer at the School of Buddhist Philosophy, Leh, Ladakh, and at Sanskrit University in Sarnath. His works include Hindi translations of Tsongkhapa's *Essence of Good Explanation of the Definitive and Interpretable* and Kamalaśīla's commentary on the *Rice Seedling Sutra*. He was the primary traditional source for the English translation of Tsongkhapa's *Great Treatise on the Stages of the Path*. He is a resident teacher at the Tibetan Buddhist Learning Center in Washington, New Jersey.

What to Read Next from Wisdom Publications

Relative Truth, Ultimate Truth
The Foundation of Buddhist Thought, Volume 2
Geshe Tashi Tsering
Edited by Gordon McDougall

"A tremendously valuable resource."—*Buddhadharma*

Insight into Emptiness
Khensur Jampa Tegchok
Edited and introduced by Thubten Chodron

"One of the best introductions to the philosophy of emptiness I have ever read."—José Ignacio Cabezón

Tsongkhapa's Praise for Dependent Relativity
Lobsang Gyatso and Graham Woodhouse

"In this elegant text, the Venerable Geshe Graham Woodhouse translates Tsongkhapa's jewel-like masterpiece. The radiance of Tsongkhapa's poetry is refracted and enhanced by the brilliant and lucid commentary of the late Gen Lobsang Gyatso."—Dr. Jay Garfield, Dorris Silbert Professor in Humanities and Professor of Philosophy at Smith College

Essence of the Vast and the Profound
A Commentary on Je Tsongkhapa's Middle-Length Treatise on the Stages of the Path to Enlightenment
Pabongka Rinpoche

"With this lucid, readable translation, David Gonsalez makes a valuable addition to the library of Buddhist translations."—Joshua W. C. Cutler, editor of *The Great Treatise on the Stages of the Path to Enlightenment*

Shantideva's Guide to Awakening
A Commentary on the Bodhicharyavatara
Geshe Yeshe Tobden

"Geshe Yeshe Tobden has that rare distinction not only of being qualified as a scholar but also of having spent many years in meditation in the mountains. As a result, his explanation has the special flavor of heartfelt personal experience." —His Holiness the Dalai Lama

The Easy Path
Illuminating the First Panchen Lama's Secret Instructions
Gyumed Khensur Lobsang Jampa
Edited by Lorne Ladner

"A marvel." —Jan Willis, author of *Dreaming Me: Black, Baptist, and Buddhist*

About Wisdom Publications

Wisdom Publications is the leading publisher of classic and contemporary Buddhist books and practical works on mindfulness. To learn more about us or to explore our other books, please visit our website at wisdomexperience.org or contact us at the address below.

Wisdom Publications
199 Elm Street
Somerville, MA 02144 USA

We are a 501(c)(3) organization, and donations in support of our mission are tax deductible.

Wisdom Publications is affiliated with the Foundation for the Preservation of the Mahayana Tradition (FPMT).